7.50

25364

D1543339

25364

# THE TASTE OF OUR TIME

*Collection planned and directed by*

**ALBERT SKIRA**

BIOGRAPHICAL AND CRITICAL STUDY

BY

ENRIQUE LAFUENTE FERRARI

*Translated by James Emmons from the French version
of the original Spanish*

# VELAZQUEZ

SKIRA

# A SILHOUETTE OF THE MAN

> "The life of Velazquez is one of the simplest a man ever lived... and... one of the most enigmatic, most difficult to understand, that is to be met with."
>
> JOSÉ ORTEGA Y GASSET.

L ESS than a year after the death of King Philip II, Velazquez was born in Seville, under the silky sky of an Andalusian summer, fragrant with jasmine and ringing with the peal of church-bells. In the popular parish of San Pedro, in the shadow of a Mudejar tower, Diego Velazquez was baptized on June 6, 1599. His father, Juan Rodriguez de Silva, came of a family of Portuguese hidalgos, native to Porto, who had settled in Seville, at that time the richest city in Spain. His mother, Jeronima Velazquez, whose name he took and made famous, was a native of Seville; she too, apparently, was of noble birth. The rank of hidalgo, a privilege of lineage, did not in itself imply the possession of wealth.

Seville was a flourishing art center. The many local schools of the 15th century had gradually come to be concentrated in a few leading cities: Toledo, the old Spanish capital, already sinking into irremediable decay; Seville, market town of a rich agricultural region and hub of overseas trade with the Americas; Valencia, the main Spanish seaport on the Mediterranean; and Madrid, seat of the monarchy under Philip II and capital of the country after 1606.

In 1610, at the age of eleven, Velazquez began his apprenticeship in the studio of the painter Francisco Pacheco, a mediocre artist but one who enjoyed great prestige in Seville; to him we owe the most interesting information we have about his young disciple. A competent, unpretentious painter, a cultivated man of letters and an art theorist, Pacheco published in Seville in 1649 a book entitled *Arte de la pintura*, a belated

LAS MENINAS, DETAIL: SELF-PORTRAIT OF VELAZQUEZ, 1656.
PRADO, MADRID.

echo of mannerist doctrines. He had read all the treatises of the Renaissance, and in his book quotations from these alternate with chapters on technique which have much to tell us about the methods and working habits of the painters of his day. Nephew of a humanist prelate, he gathered around him a circle of cultivated friends and held open house to some of the best-known poets and writers of Spain; he drew their portraits with a view to compiling a Book of Encomia, which remained unpublished in his lifetime (a facsimile edition was published in the 19th century). He was an influential man and his pupil early enjoyed the benefit of his friendships. An incidental remark dropped by Pacheco substantiates the tradition that Velazquez first studied under Francisco Herrera the Elder, a harsh, irascible man, but a bolder, more modern-minded painter than the cautious Pacheco.

When the six-year bond of apprenticeship came to an end in 1617, Velazquez passed his examination before Pacheco and the painter Juan de Uceda and qualified as a full-fledged master. A year later he married Pacheco's daughter Juana, which sufficiently testifies to the esteem in which the teacher held his disciple, and to the hopes he had founded on his talents. Pacheco must have been a better teacher than painter; he was broad-minded enough not to impose an outmoded credo on his pupil. Velazquez, for his part, had early given every sign of his bent toward a kind of painting very different from the provincial academicism of his environment. Now, a married man before his nineteenth birthday, the young artist began his professional career in the modest circumstances in which the painters of Seville lived and worked: with hopes, that is, of obtaining orders for altar pictures from the monasteries, and occasionally for portraits. But everything goes to show that he was not made for this routine. And fortune, as it so happened, was soon to favor him. Already a qualified master, though very young, he employed apprentices in his studio. Two daughters were born to him: Francisca and Ignacia. A few months after the birth of the latter occurred the event that was to change the painter's life: the accession of Philip IV to the Spanish throne.

Philip III had been a colorless, devoutly religious king, weak-willed and dull-witted; affairs of state he left in the hands of a strong man, the Duke of Lerma, thus breaking the tradition of hard work and personal government handed down by the bureaucratic king Philip II. The country had disapproved of this relinquishment of power and wished for a change. But things were not destined to change for the better. For Seville, nevertheless, the new reign began auspiciously. Philip IV, the second do-nothing king of the House of Austria, cared no more than his father for the exercise of power, and he soon left the administration in the hands of a great Sevillian nobleman, Don Gaspar de Guzman, Count-Duke of Olivares. Don Gaspar was a younger son; he was still a student at the University of Salamanca, and about to enter the Church, when the death of his elder brother made him heir to the titles and fortune of his family. As governor of the Alcazar of Seville, he paid court to the Duke of Lerma and became gentleman in waiting to the heir apparent, the future Philip IV, whose favor he soon won. This was an unmerited piece of good fortune for him, and a disaster for Spain. He was an unctuous flatterer, a bungling, incompetent administrator, but possessed with the passion for authority so common among Spanish politicians, whose main object seems to be the preservation of their own power rather than the good of the country. At the death of his uncle Don Gaspar de Zuñiga, he inherited the royal seal; soon he was prime minister, and all-powerful. He lived to witness and contribute to the final decay of the Habsburgs in Spain.

Spanish politicians have the inveterate habit—the vice—of practising favoritism on a regional basis. Around the Andalusian nobleman, now raised to power, gathered at once a whole clique of Sevillians, most of them friends of Francisco Pacheco: the poet Rioja who had acted as a witness at Velazquez' wedding; Don Luis de Fonseca, an ecclesiastic, gentleman of the king's bedchamber, and an amateur of painting; and the Alcazar brothers. Pacheco saw an opportunity here of introducing his son-in-law at court; he had faith in his talent and was well aware of his wonderful ability as a portraitist. In 1622 Velazquez paid his first visit to Madrid and gained admittance to the circle of Olivares' friends. He only succeeded in seeing the Escorial and its collections and in painting a portrait of Luis de Gongora, the great Baroque poet. The inner circles of the court were still closed to him. But a year later his luck turned. Olivares himself summoned him to Madrid. His best introduction there proved to be the portrait he made of Fonseca; the picture created a sensation in the palace. Olivares contrived to bring it to the king's attention and Philip was dazzled by the mastery of the young man from Seville. He condescended to have his own portrait painted by him; it was finished on August 30, 1623, and was a complete success. "Hitherto no one had succeeded in painting His Majesty." Velazquez was taken into the king's service, to the exclusion of all other painters, and was ordered to make his home at court.

It was not only his art, but his personal appearance, his noble birth, his simplicity, the urbanity of his manners that won over the king. For the next thirty-seven years, untiringly, Velazquez painted his royal model. Philip was the jaded scion of a dynasty blighted by interbreeding: pale and blond, as sorely averse to the business of governing as he was passionately fond of hunting, theatricals, and good-looking women. It took him twenty years to wake up to the incapacity of his prime minister and the ruinous decay of his power; when at last he tried to mend matters it was late in the day. The despotism of a single man leads to the elimination of capable statesmen; when a dictatorship reaches the end of its tether, having swept away the best men, the only ones at hand to step into the breach are fortune-hunters and makeshift politicians. If Philip IV has a title to the gratitude of posterity, he owes it to his generous patronage of Velazquez, and even more to his friendship for him. And—unusual for the Spanish court—nothing ever belied or clouded the favor Velazquez enjoyed. The king was true to his painter and never parted with him, not only employing him as a portraitist but opening to him the career of a palace official. Very high was the honor paid him, even though it encroached a little on his work as an artist. The very year of his arrival at court, the provincial master of still-life painting had as a sitter the Prince of Wales, the future Charles I of England, then on a visit to Madrid, seeking to obtain the hand of an infanta and thus to cement an alliance. Here was the heir of Queen Elizabeth soliciting the friendship of Spain! The new reign was beginning under the fairest auspices, which events, however, failed to justify.

The prompt success of the young Velazquez won him both friends and enemies. Among the most hostile to him was Vicente Carducho, an artist of Italian extraction who had been able to cut the figure of a leader at court until Velazquez arrived. He was a belated mannerist and a timid realist, more cultured than talented; he wrote some *Diálogos sobra la pintura*, published in 1633, which reveal, when read between the lines, how jealous the old academic painter was of the young revolutionary. In the early years of his official career in Madrid, Velazquez had his first —and last—taste of popular success. He had made an equestrian portrait of the king, against a landscape background, which was so much admired by all who saw it that Philip consented to have the painting exhibited in public at the gate of a monastery beside the Puerta del Sol, a singular precedent of the open-air exhibitions of today. The result was the triumph of a new manner of painting. The court poets vied with each other in singing the praises of this portrait, which has not come down to us.

This popular triumph was soon followed by the official rebuff of Velazquez' rivals in a competition organized at the palace. The new Spanish painting was now to prevail over the academicism of the Italians hitherto sponsored by the court. A historical theme was set for the competing artists to treat: the *Expulsion of the Moriscoes*, a stern political measure taken by Philip III in 1609, after the discovery of plots aimed at provoking Turkish and English reprisals. An ill-advised consequence of Spanish intolerance? In 1617 Gustavus Adolphus expelled the Catholics from Sweden, and in the matter of deportation, it is not for our time to cast the first stone. Velazquez had to compete with Carducho, Caxes and Nardi. The jury was composed of Italians, but they unhesitatingly awarded him first prize. This was in 1627. Further rewards were in store for him: in addition to small favors, the king established him on an intimate footing at court and appointed him Gentleman Usher. The provincial painter of humble still lifes, the precocious portraitist turned painter of historical pictures, now held the office that made him the king's closest confidant. Apartments were set aside for him in the palace and the king took to visiting his studio, watched him paint and chatted with him.

Rubens, court painter to the Infanta Isabella, governor of the Low Countries, came to Madrid in 1628 on an unofficial diplomatic mission. Pacheco asserts that the Flemish painter was already in correspondence with Velazquez. He now became his friend, and with him visited the Escorial and the royal collections. In their long talks together Rubens dwelt nostalgically on years spent in Italy in his youth, and filled Velazquez with

CARDINAL BORGIA, C. 1643. BLACK CHALK DRAWING.
ACADEMY OF SAN FERNANDO, MADRID.

a desire to see the marvels of Italy for himself and perfect his natural gifts by studying the Old Masters. As soon as he had put the finishing touches on his *Triumph of Bacchus*, Velazquez obtained from the king leave to travel and a grant to defray his expenses. Olivares gave him letters of recommendation to various Italian courts. The political situation in Italy just then was disturbing and the threat of war again hung over the principalities of the North. After endorsing Velazquez' passport, the Venetian ambassador took the diplomatic precaution of setting the Republic on its guard against possible spies, adding, however, that in his personal opinion the young painter's only object in going to Venice was to perfect his art. The ambassador of Parma was skeptical; he scented a political maneuver and warned his court that he suspected Velazquez of having a secret mission to fulfil.

He traveled in an official capacity, accompanying Ambrosio Spinola, the great Genoese general in the service of Spain, who died soon afterwards at the siege of Casale. Velazquez was eager to reach Venice, being attracted above all by the works of Tintoretto, several of which he copied. From Venice, by way of Ferrara, Loreto and Bologna, he went to Rome. The itinerary he followed is marked out for us by the dispatches of the Spanish ambassadors who attended him at each stage of his journey, for he was an important person at the court. In Rome he was given an apartment in the Vatican and he stayed for a time at the Villa Medici, where he brooded in the gardens among cypresses and roses. At Naples he met Ribera. Velazquez was the first Spanish artist to meet some of his greatest colleagues. He steeped himself in impressions of art and painting. These were to remain indelibly graven on the memory of the shy and silent Velazquez. Italy, which left such nostalgic associations in the mind of Cervantes, impressed itself even more deeply on this master of the visual world.

By the beginning of January 1631 he was back in Madrid. Olivares, now undisputed dictator, was playing at power politics and encouraging the amusements of the weak-willed king. The court's favorite pleasure haunt was the palace of Buen Retiro, which Olivares improved and embellished by adding to it some land of his own. Receptions, theatricals, water pageants and nocturnal entertainments followed one another in an atmosphere of obsequious flattery. Costly renovations were under way and the palace was soon filled with the works of art which his courtiers had been invited to present to the king. The great Salón de los Reinos was to be decorated with military scenes, representing Spanish feats of arms in the reign of Philip IV—it would be more exact to say in the reign of Olivares—from the Palatinate to the Americas. The duke, ostensibly flattering the king, was really preparing to glorify his own government. All the painters of any repute were set feverishly to work. Even the diffident Zurbaran, whom Velazquez had known from his prentice years, was summoned from Seville. Velazquez himself was busily painting portrait after portrait, besides a historical picture: *The Surrender of Breda*, or *The Lances*. In 1635 a chorus of court poets hymned the beauties of the country palace, the triumphs of the king, and the glorious achievements of the minister. The climax of this ill-founded optimism came with the victory won by the Infante Don Fernando, the king's brother, at the battle of Nördlingen.

Nothing could abate Philip's delight in merry-making, hunting, poetry contests, and works of art. With the Buen Retiro well enough appointed to suit his taste, he conceived the idea of decorating the Torre de la Parada, a hunting lodge in the Pardo woods. This time it was not for Spanish artists to do the work; what the king now fancied was an array of female nudes to embellish this small private retreat. The main commission went to Rubens, and with the Metamorphoses of Ovid

VIEW OF GRANADA, 1648. SEPIA DRAWING.
BIBLIOTECA NACIONAL, MADRID.

as his theme, he set his studio to work. Several rooms in the
Prado are today filled with the remains of these decorations.
Velazquez seconded the king in seeing this vast artistic program
carried out, to the detriment at times of his own work.

But things were drawing to a crisis in Spain. By the early
1640s, consistently misgoverned ever since the king had with-
drawn to Buen Retiro, the Spanish empire was shaken to its
foundations. Catalonia and Portugal were in open rebellion,
conspiracies in Andalusia and Aragon miscarried. French armies
were advancing on the Ebro. Meanwhile, Olivares was preoccupied with perpetuating his fame in an equestrian portrait

ordered from Velazquez, ostensibly to commemorate a victory won in 1639 at the defense of Fuenterrabia. The king continued to indulge in his pleasures at Buen Retiro, and one day, like a presage of evil, fire broke out in the palace. The people grew restless, and discontent spread. The economic situation was ruinous. Not even the king's household could make ends meet. Salaries were overdue. We find Velazquez claiming arrears for paintings finished and delivered. As early as 1630 an Italian ambassador at Madrid could write: "The King pays no one."

Velazquez married off his daughter in 1634, and from then on, in the person of his son-in-law Mazo, he had an able assistant to relieve him of routine work and the replicas so often requested of him. His official duties at the palace occupied the bulk of his time. Yet he painted steadily, mostly portraits, countless portraits, for presentation to foreign courts. In acknowledgment of his services, his salary was raised in 1637.

The hour of decision had come. Condé's victory at Rocroy dealt a fatal blow to Spanish arms and Olivares' position became untenable. The war in Catalonia obliged the king to bestir himself to the extent of inspecting his troops in the field in 1642. Velazquez accompanied him to Saragossa. But the situation got no better, and by 1643 Philip had no alternative but to dismiss Olivares.

Velazquez' position was unaffected by the disgrace of the man who had first patronized him. The king esteemed him as a friend and fresh responsibilities devolved upon him. Again he accompanied his master into Aragon and Catalonia, and at Fraga in 1644 he painted one of his finest portraits of him. They were traveling again in 1645 and 1646. Appointed Gentleman of the Bedchamber, his new duties required his constant attendance on the king. In 1645 Lerida was recaptured, but in the following year Sicily revolted; and, what was worse, Prince Don Baltasar Carlos died, the king's eldest son and heir to the throne, the last hope of the dynasty, an intelligent boy of great promise, of whom Velazquez had made such charming portraits. Revolt broke out in Naples. The world seemed to be collapsing around the king. The Peace of Westphalia in 1648 was the first open admission of the decay of Spanish power.

Philip IV consoled himself with comedies and painting. Had he not been a king, he would have been a poet, a collector, a lover of life; he had the makings of an artist; as a king he was a failure and the undoing of his country. As he made plans to form a picture gallery, Velazquez volunteered to go to Italy and buy the masterpieces of painting and statuary which would give new luster to the royal collections. Letters were dispatched to the Spanish ambassadors at Italian courts recommending Velazquez to their care and protection. He sailed from Malaga in 1649, joining on board ship the official mission headed by the Duke of Najera, bound for Trent to fetch the new Austrian wife of the king, who was anxious to provide an heir to his throne. Landing at Genoa on February 11, Velazquez parted company with the embassy and proceeded to revisit the cities that had captivated him twenty years before: Milan, Padua, Venice, Modena, Rome, Naples.

Received in Venice as the king's envoy and a notability, known to have come in search of major works of art, he was attended on and paid homage to. He was even "interviewed" —a Baroque interview, befitting the times, and in verse, written in the Venetian dialect and included by Marco Boschini in his book *La Carta del Navegar pitoresco*, published in Venice years later in 1660. Here is the description it gives of Velazquez:

*Cavalier, che spirava un gran decoro*
*Quanto ogn'altra autorevole persona.*

A cavalier breathing as great a dignity
As any other person of authority.

The gravity and natural distinction of a man who had gone through the hard school of palace life are reflected in these lines. But what interested Boschini were the painter's personal opinions. And to make these agreeable to a Venetian, the Spaniard had no need to force himself. He passionately admired Tintoretto and extolled above all the *Glory* in the Ducal Palace, of which he was lucky enough to acquire a sketch, now in the Prado. Then Boschini put the inevitable question: "What about Raphael?" To this Velazquez replied with unabashed sincerity, admitting that he disliked him:

> "*Rafael (a dire il vero,*
> *Piasendome esser libero e sincero)*
> *Stago perdir, che nol mi piase niente.*"
> "Raphael (truth to tell,
> And I choose to be frank and sincere)
> I was about to say I do not care for."

He made no secret of his views on art and the Venetian "reporter" thus set them down in verse:

> "*A Venetia si trova el bon, e 'l belo*
> *Mi, dago il primo luogo a quel penelo,*
> *Tizian xe quel che porta la bandiera.*"
> "In Venice the good and beautiful are found,
> For my part I give first place to this brush,
> Titian it is who bears the banner."

So Velazquez, with the courage of his convictions, was not afraid to differ with orthodox opinions of Italian art. And he acted—that is to say he bought—accordingly. The pictures of Tintoretto, Veronese and Titian thus acquired by Velazquez are today the pride of the Prado. On his way to Naples he stopped in Rome, replenished his purse, and saw that the royal orders for works of art were properly filled. After seeing Ribera at Naples he returned to Rome and there met many artists: Bernini, Salvator Rosa, Pietro di Cortona. One wonders whether he may not have met Poussin; the two men were so different temperamentally, one French, the other Spanish, one a rationalist, the other an existentialist, that they could hardly have taken to each other.

The reputation of Velazquez, his mission and the trust placed in him by the King of Spain, won him the great honor of painting the pope. Innocent X, of the Doria Pamphili family, offered a thankless subject for a painter anxious to idealize his model, but Velazquez was more than equal to the task. As the artist had been out of practice for the past year, he first made a trial portrait, to "warm up" his hand, of his servant Juan de Pareja. The portrait of Pareja won him a public triumph: exhibited at the Pantheon on March 19, 1650, it was more admired than any of the other works on view. The Roman painters paid homage to his prodigious skill. Velazquez was elected a member of the Academy of St Luke, and then the pope sat to him. The result was a quickly, freely brushed portrait that spread his fame abroad. He declined any remuneration, and could only be prevailed on to accept a gold chain as a personal mark of esteem from the Holy Father. The pope's whole entourage insisted on having their portraits painted in turn: his sister-in-law Olympia Maidalchini, who reigned over the papal court, Cardinal Astalli-Pamphili, the Monsignori of the chamber, and even the pope's barber. Velazquez also painted one of his colleagues, the woman painter Flaminia Trionfi. Except for the pope's and the cardinal's portraits, all these works have been lost.

He turned now to the errand on which he had come: the acquisition of statues and casts. Day after day he visited Roman collections and enjoyed to the full life in the papal city. But his king was growing impatient. He missed Velazquez and instructed his ambassadors to hasten his return. Velazquez had been due back in Madrid in June 1650. The Duke of L'Infantado, Spanish ambassador in Rome, received pointed orders from the king to arrange for the painter's return journey. "You know his phlegmatic nature," wrote Philip. "See that he does not take advantage of it to protract his sojourn at that court (i.e. in Rome)." But Velazquez was not to be hurried, and lingered on for another year. Five letters summoning him home were written by the king to his ambassador. The painter toyed with the idea of returning by way of Paris, but the wars then in progress made the journey hazardous and he had to give it up. In June 1651, a year behind schedule, he landed at Barcelona. He was never granted another leave of absence.

Work in abundance was waiting for him at the Alcazar. First came the exacting, unremitting task of painting portraits. In his absence a new queen had arrived at court; portraits had to be made of her and of the young Infanta, Maria Teresa, whose hand, when the time for marriage came, might be a diplomatic asset. Children were soon to be born to the ill-matched royal couple, and portraits of them had accordingly to be sent to foreign courts, as family presents, and to show that the future of the dynasty was assured. In the nine years left him to live, Velazquez produced an immense body of work. He was awarded the highest honors and multiplied his titles to glory. It fell to him too, as to the curator of a museum in our day, to install the works of art he had brought back from Italy. The royal galleries could then boast of fabulous collections, of which those now in the Prado are only the remains. With the works for which no room could be found in the royal palace of Madrid, Velazquez organized another museum in the lower halls of the Escorial.

As time went on, the king looked upon him more and more as a trusted friend. When the post of Marshal of the Royal Household fell vacant in 1652, various candidates came forward and the council of high palace functionaries submitted its proposals to the king. No one placed the name of Velazquez at the head of the list of persons recommended; most of them added it at the end, a few gave it the next to last place; only one made bold to place it second. The king sent back the list with these words in the margin: "I appoint Velazquez." The post incurred heavy obligations and involved him in a maze of bureaucratic procedures: he had to take charge of the Privy Chamber, give orders, keep accounts, humor pride and vanity, and observe etiquette and precedence. His composure and self-possession enabled him to bear up under it all with philosophic detachment. He found relief from the petty vanities of the living in the silent friendship of the dead and the contemplation of their works. Titian, Tintoretto, Veronese, El Greco and Rubens, whose pictures hung in the galleries of the Alcazar, consoled him for the intrigues of his gilded prison. Sometimes he shut himself away in his studio, to commune with his own painting. And as always he found escape in nature, accompanying the king on his visits to the royal residences and on his hunting expeditions, beneath the shade trees of Aranjuez and the leafy vaults of the Pardo forest or the Valsain woods. In the distance, rising tier on tier, the blue-tinged heights of the Sierra de Guadarrama. One listens for the strains of a pavane by Ravel at the thought of that court, with its faded old king, full of sin and remorse, the ladies in farthingales, the courtiers, the nun-like duennas, the gamboling of dogs and dwarfs.

In 1658 the king took an even bolder step: he made Velazquez a Knight of Santiago, an inestimable title of nobility in that proud, caste-conscious society, exclusively preoccupied with prerogatives and privileges. Painters applauded, the aristocrats shook their heads. A dauber of canvases placed on an equal footing with the noblest Castilians! Still, it was not so easy to qualify. Velazquez' pedigree and estate had to be minutely inquired into by a royal commission; it had to be proved, and attested by witnesses, that his lineage was pure on both sides of the house, and furthermore that the exercise of painting had never been for him a mercenary profession. The salary he received from the king was discounted, for to serve his royal highness was an honor, not an employment; to the king he did not sell, he presented his pictures. The records of the commission contain the kindly, sometimes complaisant statements of aristocrats, knights of various orders, and friends of Velazquez' youth at Seville: Zurbaran, Alonso Cano, Nardi. The keeper of the royal records, Don Gaspar de Fuensalida, added that he "had always known him in the palace, in the king's service, as the greatest painter there was, and had ever been in Europe, according to the testimony of Rubens himself." To conclude the proceedings the pope's approbation was required. At length it came, and Velazquez was invested with the habit of the Order of Santiago in July 1659. He had but one year to live.

Honors and rank, yes, but how poor the reality behind them! A few months later we find the painter of the chamber and personal friend of the king claiming the arrears of his salary and informing the palace comptroller that the staff were being increasingly demoralized by the mismanagement of affairs: "Worst of all is this," he added, "that there is not a real to be had to pay for the wood in the fireplaces of His Majesty's chamber." Disheartening penury, accounts behind-hand, endless paperwork, spite and jealousy from courtiers, but also confidence and friendship from the king, and an incomparable series of paintings—such is the strange and somber picture we get of Velazquez' last years.

It was left for him to shine in the ranks of the Spanish nobility on the last occasion on which the Austrian monarchy displayed, almost as its swan-song, the pomp of its solemn etiquette. The struggle between France and Spain for supremacy in Europe, two centuries old, was drawing to a close. Philip IV had sued for peace, and in 1659 was signed the treaty known to history as the Peace of the Pyrenees. To put the seal on it Philip consented to the marriage in the following year of his daughter Maria Teresa to Louis XIV of France, the rising star, the future Roi Soleil. The marriage ceremony took place in the Isle of Pheasants, in the Bidassoa, on the frontier of the two countries, in the presence of the two kings. As Marshal of the Royal Household, Velazquez preceded the king in order to see the living quarters prepared and the pavilions decorated. He left for Fuenterrabia on April 7, 1660. The state of his health must even then have been precarious, for, unusual with him, he traveled in a litter. The historic meeting of the kings took place. In order to provide a setting worthy of the occasion, Velazquez had had the pavilions hung with the finest tapestries from the splendid royal collections. Moving among princes, ministers, grandees and great ladies, Velazquez performed his functions with consummate tact and innate distinction, with the éclat and self-assurance that his recent elevation had given him.

Then, like an evil omen, the rumor spread in Madrid that he had died on the journey. When he reached home on June 26, the anxiety and distress of his family and friends were dispelled. But not for long. A hidden disorder combined with the fatigue of the journey had begun to tell on him. "... *labore itineraris febri prehendus...*" reads the epitaph composed at his death. On July 31 the disease declared itself, sudden and violent. The king dispatched his own physicians, to no avail. On August 6, 1660, in the royal annex called the Casa del Tesoro, where he had painted his finest works, Velazquez died. The next day, escorted by a solemn procession of courtiers dressed in the habit of the order of knighthood to which he had lately been raised, the painter of Philip IV was interred in the church of St John the Baptist near the Alcazar. A few days later, faithful even to the rendezvous with death, Juana Pacheco was united to her husband in the tomb.

Of the king's grief we have a brief but eloquent testimony. Velazquez had been prevented by death from settling the accounts of his office. Bureaucratic routine takes no notice of mourning. Nine days after the painter's death a memorandum was submitted to the king calling for the reimbursement, in the State's favor, of fees received by Velazquez. Philip IV felt the indelicacy of this procedure. His thoughts turned to his deceased friend and, on the document that had revived his grief for the loss of so great a painter, he wrote these words which do him honor: "I am overwhelmed."

★

The life of Velazquez, with its background of artistic genius and its melancholy façade, unfolded like a dream within the walls of the royal palace. A clear, upright, unmysterious life as regards all the official, outward events referred to in the documents; but beyond that it is almost impossible to penetrate. Very seldom are we afforded a glimpse behind the closed door of his private life. What was he like in the integrity of his personality, in his inner reactions? Something of his character transpires in the few phrases he uttered which have come down to us; and reading between the lines, as best we can, of contemporary texts dealing with him, we may perhaps succeed in sketching out a picture of the man.

In his prentice years at Seville, Pacheco noted "his virtue, his rectitude, his happy penchants." "Good nature, noble blood," wrote Palomino. Andalusians are accounted resourceful, fickle, boastful. Velazquez was a staid, silent, serious-minded young man who went his own way, knew what he had to do, and did it. No hesitations, no influences. Steadfast, disconcerting self-confidence, with that aloofness shown by certain taciturn Andalusians. At the bottom of his soul Velazquez found his spiritual sustenance in his own superiority, but he never let this be felt by others, because his distinction of mind forbade him to do so. This superiority at once commanded the respect of his teacher, who acknowledged it in his book: "I do not esteem it discreditable that the pupil should surpass the master." Praiseworthy attitude for a man as possessed by his science and his learning as Pacheco was; it does honor to him as much as to his pupil. We know well enough that young painters in art schools readily undergo the influence of talented fellow students whose work announces the style of the day, and this explains the fact that the nascent fame of the prodigiously gifted adolescent who was painting "new things" quickly spread to all the studios in Seville. So it is that he very early came in contact with several apprentices who later became famous: Zurbaran and Alonso Cano, whose lifelong friend he remained. One hesitates to imagine him a gay and sociable comrade. Yet the imprint of the Sevillian genius seldom fails to make itself felt even in the gravest sons of that city. And that imprint is stamped on the rare, pithy, pertinent phrases from Velazquez' mouth which have been preserved. In Madrid he was nicknamed "El Sevillano," thus linking the memory of his birthplace to the course of his whole life. He never lost the delicate accent of his native province in his manner of speaking Castilian. One of his autograph signatures shows that he used the Andalusian *s* instead of the Castilian *z*, a slip still common today among natives of Andalusia.

At twenty-four he left his provincial studio for the Alcazar of the king of Spain, where he spent the rest of his life. What a difficult test this change was, and what a feather in the cap of a vain man so precocious a success might have been. But his equanimity, his nobility of character, preserved Velazquez from these dangers. He retained his self-possession and peace of mind, showed no surprise at his good fortune and took life as it came. Not only the known facts of his career make this clear, but also his work. He breathed the sweet incense of glory without losing his head. His lucid mind and powers of observation very soon enabled him, on the contrary, to see through the web of intrigue and scheming that generally distinguishes a court. And what a court! Turn to the literature of the period: Quevedo lashes at a Madrid of time-servers, petitioners, unsalaried soldiers, schemers, adventurers back from America, haughty nobles, and a whole rout of superstitious, picaresque hangers-on living on their wits and fawning on grandees.

An idle king stood somewhere far above them, like a myth, and it was given to very, very few to reach him. He sympathized at once with his young painter. He treated him with affection, esteem, friendliness, and admired him. This was too much for the envious, pretentious, mediocre painters of the court, who would have none of him. Carducho's *Diálogos* are full of anonymous pin-pricks aimed at the newcomer: the great painters had never been portraitists; the important thing was not sleight of hand, but imagination and abidance by an ideal composition; the secret of art lay not in color, but in design; the painter who contents himself with the natural was like the play-actor who recites lines written by others; imitation was mere empiricism; painting could be good even if ill-colored, and so on. Velazquez must have been for Carducho "that monster of dexterity and naturalness," devoid of precepts and doctrine, to whom he alludes in his book. The ideal, the doctrine, for this the old mannerist yearned with academic nostalgia. The disregard of principles in the new manner of painting would, he foretold, prove to be the ruin of art, whose doom was already presaged in still lifes of abject meanness and low-mindedness, and in pictures of topers and good-for-nothings. Here was a direct attack. Proof again that there is nothing new under the sun; these pessimistic lamentations have broken out anew at each stylistic crisis in art history.

Velazquez went his way undeterred, reasserting his self-confidence in terse rejoinders, as always a man of few words. He would rather, he said, be first in his rough manner than second in an affected mannerism. One day, the king having said to him, "They claim that heads are the only thing you know how to paint," he replied, "This is a great honor, Sire, for hitherto I have never seen a head well painted." In Italy he expressed his opinion of Raphael with the same frankness with which El Greco told Pacheco in Toledo that Michelangelo was a good fellow, but unfortunately did not know how to paint.

Ortega y Gasset has singled out and emphasized Velazquez' aspiration to the nobility, which he considered the key to his character. Even while making due allowance for the prejudices of the age, I cannot believe that the mainspring of his career is to be sought for in such an ambition. Velazquez, as Boschini acknowledges, was a man of noble nature, noble bearing, noble manners. His reserve tinged with aloofness, his uneffusive generosity and warm, unostentatious kindness won him, in spite of the enmity a superior man is bound to arouse, the sincere attachment of many excellent friends. Witness the fifty-nine persons of quality who testified in his favor during the inquiry preceding his nomination to the Order of Santiago. Even when he had reached the highest offices, the petty vexations of his colleagues and of the palace administration failed to touch him. He knew nothing of adulation, backbiting, intrigue. The man who painted those landscapes of blue mountains bathed in gray light could only have been a contemplative spirit, a lover of solitude, shut in the world of his own meditations. The king's esteem sustained him. Philip IV liked to repair to his studio and watch him paint; and a chair was at all times reserved there for him. Through the windows of the gallery of the Cierzo (north wind) streamed the pure light of the Castilian plateau, and the sun that tempered its cold winters and went down in splendor. In those quiet hours at his easel, how could Velazquez have been otherwise than happy? His vision was so keen that, as soon as he had laid in the essential, he lost any concern with putting a smooth finish on the picture. He worked at his own rhythm, quite dispassionately, with an elegant economy of means, as Andalusians generally do. Then he left his studio for the business of the antechamber: accounts, reports and memoranda from the keeper of the records and the comptroller, surveillance of work in progress, and tedious minutiae. The most congenial of his duties was no doubt the fitting up of the king's new residences, the hanging of pictures by the great masters which had to harmonize with the decorations, had to balance and complement each other. Here a golden-tinted Titian, there a green-flushed Tintoretto; a little further on, opulent nudes by Rubens; in a ceremonial hall, portraits by Moro and Coello. An idea of the refinement of his taste may be had from an incidental remark of Palomino, who describes the care with which Velazquez chose his costume for the solemn meeting of the Infanta and Louis XIV: "As for the color of the cloth, one had to admire how well it suited him, for he was superior in his knowledge of materials and always showed great taste in choosing them."

Of his private life we know nothing more. A quiet home, a faithful, loving wife, a married daughter whose children brightened the house. A son-in-law who was at once a disciple and assistant. An uneventful, unadventurous artist's life, whose leisurely rhythm gave him time to enjoy it to the full. An existence unattended by anecdote or eccentricity, but answering to a profound sense of serenity and peace. The confessions of Velazquez are in his works. Praising one of his pictures, a poet of the day coined this apt expression: "The soul breathes out through his brush."

A noble soul, a proud spirit. Thus Velazquez appears to us.

# LIFE FIRST OF ALL

"And because your perfections, Lord, were infinite,
and a single creature could not embody them all, it was
necessary to create many in order for each, for its part,
piecemeal, to reveal something of all."

FRAY LUIS DE GRANADA.

FEW painters have been as impervious as Velazquez to what
are called influences. For a young artist beginning his career
it is difficult indeed to escape the environment in which he
and his masters were schooled. But from the outset Velazquez
drew on his own resources. He broke radically with what was
current practice in the studios of his day. The painters of
Seville were then producing enormous altar pictures, whose
composition was heavy and redundant, whose figures were
conventional; these works purported to echo the grandiose
monumentality of the Italian painters, but were in reality no
more than a naive and clumsy reflection of them.

This was provincial art, with a certain bravura of handling
in the work of Herrera, with brilliant color effects in that of
Roelas. None of this could have any interest for Velazquez,
except when temperament broke through convention. Herrera
the Elder, for example, showed flashes of a new painting;
hence the importance of Velazquez' brief apprenticeship in
his studio. Herrera was a vehement, short-tempered man, and
a harsh taskmaster, and if Palomino is to be believed, his pupils
could never bear with him very long. From the same author
we learn that Velazquez stayed but a short time, which indicates
his precocity, for he was only eleven when he entered Pacheco's
studio. With his bold brushwork, his rich impasto, his sober
palette and ochre tonalities, Herrera undoubtedly had some
weight in the formation of Velazquez. At the very least, he
must be given credit for feeling and responding to the imperative

of his time, its "need of prose," and so he abandoned now and then the "great machines" of his religious works for still lifes which deserved the renown they won.

When Velazquez began to make a name for himself with his still lifes, Herrera must have claimed the honor of having shown him the way. Pacheco's jealousy was aroused and, without naming Herrera, he waxes indignant in his book that anyone else should dare to arrogate that glory to himself. The point at issue would be unimportant, were we not bound to acknowledge that Velazquez' early works, his delineations of kitchens and studies from life, are closer to Herrera than to Pacheco, whose re-echoes of Michelangelo savored too much of theory to be anything but discouraging to a young painter.

Unconsciously, but resolutely, the apprentice turned away from those vast, futile compositions, which today fill the largest rooms in Seville Museum; he insisted on reinserting painting in the only element that attracted him—in immersing it, that is, in the current of life. This he resolved to do. In view of this new approach to painting, it matters relatively little whether or not in his youth Velazquez saw any pictures by Caravaggio. The latter, in spite of his overwrought gesticulations, his violent light effects and all the stock devices of Baroque composition which he used, is indeed, as Zahn has said, "the last of the classics." The first fruits of Velazquez' art, and even more the guiding purpose which led him to paint as he did, were very different.

The few details Pacheco gives us of his pupil's ways show how independent he was of his master, and how surprised the latter was at his tastes. "While still a child," writes Pacheco, "he used to pay a little peasant to serve him as a model in different postures and actions, crying or laughing, without shirking any difficulty." This means that the copying of classical models from prints held little or no interest for him.

THE OLD COOK, 1617-1622.
THE NATIONAL GALLERY OF SCOTLAND, EDINBURGH.

He found life itself more appealing—the forms of objects, the qualities of color, everything we perceive visually, whose marrow has to be extracted to make a work of art. Beauty, for him, was not a disembodied ideal but the concrete reality of existence; if, from that raw material, an artist can distil the quintessence, he will succeed in making a work of art, for beauty consists not in juxtaposing natural forms around an idea artificially inspired by the complacent admiration of antiquity, but in working out an expressive, sensuous figuration grounded in reality. What we thus define in an *a posteriori* synthesis was for Velazquez purely a matter of lucid intuition. Life itself, unalloyed with the stuff of dreams or phantasmagoria, was the first term and condition of success. This was Velazquez' self-imposed point of departure in his simple and modest acceptance of reality: objects and persons, first of all, uncompromisingly and truthfully represented. This was not the end but the means to an end.

The painter opened his eyes on what was in front of him: a peasant, his model, or a kitchen-maid. In the foreground, a table whose nuances and shadows the studio light enabled him to capture, and on which objects stood out singly in all the sharpness of their form and texture. The dull glow of earthenware, the golden crust of bread, the transparency of glasses, the downy skin of fruit, the flickering gleams of copper, what modest wonders! Giving himself up to the delineation of them, as if training himself to record real, tangible life at close range, Velazquez, a nominalist without realizing it, discovered the visual beauty of the world. It is true that, generally speaking, the Baroque age took an interest in the theme of still life, lending itself as it does to displays of technical wizardry and color effects. But how different are Velazquez' interiors in conception and pictorial quality from the virtuoso execution and gaudy butcher's stalls of the Flemings and Italians! What Velazquez painted in this line remains, rather, within the sober, austere tradition, intimate and concentrated, of Fray Juan Sanchez Cotan, the painter of Toledo whose still lifes are so steeped in poetry and humility, in an accentuated chiaroscuro, and who was active around 1600, at a time when the innovations of Caravaggio were as yet unknown in Spain.

THE WATER CARRIER OF SEVILLE, 1618-1620.
WELLINGTON MUSEUM, APSLEY HOUSE, LONDON.

Chance, as a rule, is responsible for the anthology of a given body of work bequeathed to us by the past. If we assume that a painter's logical evolution—reality, however, is not necessarily logical—is from the simple to the complex, then we should consider Velazquez' earliest Sevillian works to be those which appear least crowded and which are treated as studies rather than finished pictures. Into this category would come the two versions of *The Servant* (Art Institute of Chicago and Sir Alfred Beit Collection, London) and the *Two Young Men at Table* (Apsley House, London). On the other hand, and this too carries weight in establishing a chronology, the two versions of *Peasants at Table* (Budapest and Leningrad) are the pictures which seem to come closest to the painting of Herrera the Elder. These are the most naive and variegated of his works, and on this account should no doubt be regarded as the earliest in date. The two versions of *The Servant* and the pictures immediately following them already evince the serenity and peace which were soon to characterize the whole of his work; they are truly imbued with the painter's spirit. "He liked to drill himself in studying the expressions of the human face," Pacheco tells us. Taking this as a touchstone, the first pictures in which laughing figures appear, caught in lively, unguarded attitudes, might be held to be the earliest works, as this anecdotal attitudinizing was soon to give way to gravity and reserve.

The two pictures of *Peasants at Table* mentioned above and the Havana *Vintager* (if this is really by Velazquez) would show him entering on the path he followed after the *Servants*. The *Musical Trio* in Berlin stands out among Velazquez' early works owing to a more plastic execution, polished forms, volumes dry and stiff as cardboard, and the presence of elements which may be considered Caravaggesque. But except for the smiling boy and the table in perspective, the folded napkins, the boy's hand in the immediate foreground, the nodding of heads, and the bend of the arm holding the violin are already features peculiar to Velazquez.

The cleaning of the London *Servant* has revealed a distant representation of Christ at Emmaus in the upper lefthand corner. The same device occurs in the more mature painting of *Christ in the House of Martha* (National Gallery, London). Whether this is meant to be an actual scene glimpsed outside the room or a painted picture hung on the wall is not clear. The ambiguity is intentional on Velazquez' part. It conveys his aloofness from the theme, a certain bashfulness before the religious subject, for fear perhaps of lapsing into conventional rhetoric and so departing from life. There can be no doubt that the girl with mortar and pestle in *Christ in the House of Martha* is the same as the one portrayed in another scene, simpler in composition, which is now at Santa Monica, California, and which must be numbered among Velazquez' very earliest works. The transition toward this deepening insight into visible reality is to be found, I think, in *The Old Cook* (National Gallery of Scotland, Edinburgh).

The most momentous innovation of all these pictures lies in the intensification of certain presences, rendered immediately perceptible by the abnormal disposition of the foreground seen from above. The cinema has accustomed our eyes to a heightening of expressive values in the foreground. This shift of emphasis, which Velazquez discovered while still a youth, is both physical and psychic. Seen from this angle, which is not that of either ordinary or academic vision, things acquire a force which compensates for the humble purposes they usually serve. Here was a radical novelty: the simplest objects of daily life, valued by the painter for their qualities of form and texture, move into the foreground while all the rest becomes secondary, including the religious theme, in some pictures a mere allusion.

THE OLD COOK (DETAIL), 1617-1622.
THE NATIONAL GALLERY OF SCOTLAND, EDINBURGH.

THE WATER CARRIER OF SEVILLE (DETAIL), 1618-1620.
WELLINGTON MUSEUM, APSLEY HOUSE, LONDON.

Eggs frying in oil, or a large earthenware jar distorted by high perspective, these become the center of focus and, in Velazquez' hands, rise to the top of the hierarchy of picture elements. There had been nothing like this even in Caravaggio, and at the sight of this innovation the academic painters of the day, who considered still life to be the lowest, most vulgar form of painting, could only brand it as an aberration.

Velazquez rose in quick stages toward the mastery of his art. He achieved it to the full in the *Water Carrier of Seville*. Here his intention was consciously carried out, and the stage of the "nature piece" is superseded in this flawless composition, which contains much more than mere appearances. The point is that Velazquez always disdains anecdote and goes straight to the painting. His canvas is first of all a play of volumes whose fully rounded plasticity delights him: a jug in the very forefront, a jar, and a glass of transparent crystal; then curved forms caressed by the eye and the brush, with the diagonal rhythm of three heads set off against the penumbra; lastly, a barely inflected diagonal, formed by the fold of the leading figure's smock, subdues the rhythm of volumes and curves. The humanization and unruffled peace of this work come to bear on this point, slightly off-center, on which attention is focused: the meeting of hands and glass which introduces something almost ritual into this trivial scene. The judicious color scheme is in no way inferior. Two bright notes descend along a diagonal, the water carrier's sleeve and the boy's collar, while a whole scale of earth colors is orchestrated in the penumbra.

Parallel with this production, Velazquez had to pursue a necessary and not overly enthusiastic initiation into religious painting. His *Immaculate Virgin* and *St John the Baptist*, both treated as hard volumes, in dark flesh tints, are like figures carved in wood. The *Supper at Emmaus* in New York offers

CHRIST IN THE HOUSE OF MARTHA (DETAIL), 1617-1619. REPRODUCED
BY COURTESY OF THE TRUSTEES, THE NATIONAL GALLERY, LONDON.

a characteristic alliance of a pious subject and a popular atmosphere. The animation of the apostles' gestures comes as a surprise, even though it is called for by the theme. The picture has suffered a good deal, but I believe it to be by Velazquez' hand and I know for a fact that copies of it existed at Seville. The *Adoration of the Magi* in the Prado is, to my mind, a maturer work because here his approach to the religious theme proceeds directly from life. From now on the artist confronts all the themes he sets out to paint, religious, mythological or historical, by freeing himself from the idealizing conventions of the Renaissance and Mannerist tradition, or better, as Ortega y Gasset put it, by "reducing the subject to its logarithm of reality." In the case of the Prado *Adoration*, the theme becomes more accessible because reduced in effect to the theme of a family picture. The work is signed and I believe the date should be read as 1619. In that year, having recently married, Velazquez had a daughter. The birth of the child, the woman penetrated with her motherhood, the homage paid by the onlookers, the miracle wrought afresh by each new appearance of life, all this is in the picture and also arose at that time out of the personal experience of Velazquez himself. The tonality is yellowish brown, but carmines and pale greens begin to appear, indicating an enrichment of his palette. Whether or not he took his wife as a model, Velazquez saw the Virgin through Juana de Miranda, and Jesus beneath the features of the child born, or about to be born, to him. Models also appear in this picture who recur in all his work of this period. The composition presents the same pattern of organization: a crossing of diagonals. Its center of focus is the marvelous head of the Child, quivering with life. Patches of light and shade are balanced intentionally and not allowed to alter the forms of figures arbitrarily. Channeled by the light, attention is brought to bear on the group of Mother and Child and centered on the essential point, which gives its

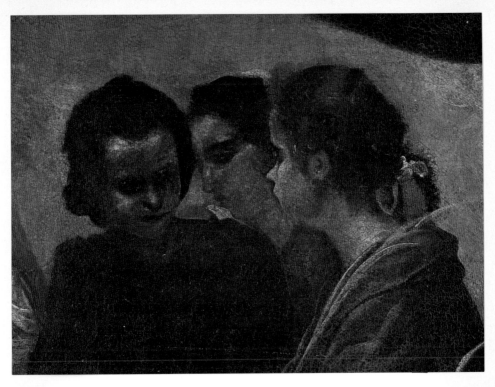

ST ILDEFONSO RECEIVING THE CHASUBLE FROM THE VIRGIN (DETAIL), 1623.
ARCHBISHOP'S PALACE, SEVILLE.

significance to the picture: the hand of the kneeling king
offering his gifts. Here skill is seconded by the painter's instinct
and not by the academic precedents revered by his teacher.

Referring to the discipline Velazquez imposed on himself in
the study of nature, Pacheco says that in this way he "achieved
sureness in portraiture." And it is true that Velazquez was
passionately attracted by the thing that stood in front of him,

ST ILDEFONSO RECEIVING THE CHASUBLE FROM THE VIRGIN, 1623.
ARCHBISHOP'S PALACE, SEVILLE.

whether being or object, man or jar. How could he help being attracted by portraits too? The ones he painted while still at Seville have the same pictorial force, the same clean-cut plasticity, the same yellowish brown tonality as his still lifes and religious pictures. Such are the portrait of Cristobal Suarez de Ribera with, for the first time, a lyrical glimpse of a landscape; the head in the Prado supposed to represent Pacheco; and above all the impressive effigy in the Prado of the nun of Toledo who, at sixty-five, wasted and wrinkled by so many years of enclosure, sailed from Seville to found a convent at Manilla. All these works—together with a sequence of apostles of which a few are extant—must have been painted before 1622, when Velazquez paid his first visit to Madrid. The portrait of Gongora (Boston Museum), executed then, links up directly with the earlier portraits. The nun and the poet are alike in their tremendous energy. Velazquez plumbs the model and reveals its character to us with impressive force, the force of life itself.

What a breath of novelty stirs too in the strange picture of *St Ildefonso receiving the Chasuble from the Virgin*, now in the Archbishop's Palace of Seville. This is a resolute and at the same time almost too naïve attempt to express the allusion to a supernatural world. The solution adopted is unusual in the School of Seville, hitherto accustomed to treat the subject on a large scale and to leave a respectable distance between heaven and earth. This is only hinted at here by a few solid gray clouds which barely rise above the ground on which the saint is kneeling. I am inclined to believe that this picture was painted after his first visit to Madrid and his first sight of paintings by El Greco, whose clouds have some similarity with those painted by Velazquez, but here the resemblance ends. The Virgin and her companions inhabiting these unusual clouds are also taken from life; they are, quite literally, girls of Seville, as their features and coiffure make plain. The only thing missing is a flower in their hair. Yet this ingenuous picture is by no means trivial. Its force of execution saves it from lapsing into anecdote and Velazquez' method asserts its authority: a total concentration on the reality of the saint's head—light and life—and on the feminine hands which grant him their gift.

The youthful stage of Velazquez' work thus draws to a close. An almost magical change was about to come over the artist's life. But in the process of adapting himself to the new tasks awaiting him in a very different milieu, it is safe to say that he found it greatly to his advantage now to have repudiated, from the very first, the Mannerist ambience and academic convention. To find his authentic and original expression, he had thus been free at the outset to go straight to life. And this harsh and passionate contact henceforth enabled him, without surrendering anything of himself, to approach kings and freaks, great captains and adventurers, infantas and gods, with the same freedom.

# PAINTER TO THE KING

*"We painters, however lowly our station may be, are yet able to confer a favor even on kings."*

PALOMINO.

WHEN Fonseca summoned Velazquez to a court dominated by the influence of Olivares, the painter's life took a decisive turn. The shy provincial suddenly found himself, at twenty-four, moving among the high and mighty of the earth. A fairy's wand touched Velazquez' head and the world changed from what it was. The king at once fell under the spell of this young man, nearly of his own age, who was master of so prodigious an art. It was a stroke of luck for Velazquez that, with Antonio Moro, Sanchez Coello and Pantoja de la Cruz, the Spanish court had grown accustomed to a severe style of portraiture devoid of mundane pomp and courtly flattery. For the genuine Spaniard, man comes before social hierarchies, before power or money—flesh-and-blood man, who lives, says Unamuno, on the hunger of immortality. For him, over and above any functions, any social role or duties, stands the human person; and this is the greatness and the limitation of his condition as a Spaniard. As Americo Castro has said, the integrity of the human person is the essential value for this hard and ascetic people, accustomed to glory and poverty, to exaltation and renunciation.

Neither the first effigy Velazquez painted of his king nor the equestrian portrait exhibited in 1625 on the steps of the monastery of San Felipe has been preserved. His earliest extant court portraits are those of Philip IV (Metropolitan Museum, New York) and Olivares (Sao Paulo Museum), both painted in 1624 to the order of Doña Antonia Ipeñarrieta; the receipts of her payments signed by Velazquez himself still exist, and thus ironically belie the obliging statements of the painter's

PORTRAIT OF LUIS DE GONGORA, 1622.
MUSEUM OF FINE ARTS, BOSTON.

friends who, when the king nominated him to the Order of Santiago, testified on oath that Velazquez had never taken money for his pictures (this was the condition of his elevation to the knighthood).

The authenticity of these two portraits has been challenged, but I believe groundlessly; both are well documented. In 1624, moreover, the artist could scarcely have had any disciples in Madrid familiar with his manner and capable of producing such perfect replicas. One cannot help noticing that in these portraits Velazquez was experiencing some difficulty in adapting himself to his new tasks. He failed as yet to dominate the silhouette and did not pose the figure as he was soon to do. Indeed, with the full-length portrait of Philip IV in the Prado and thereafter, we find him making rapid progress, visible notably in the correction of the awkward, compass-like arrangement of the legs. This is one of the first examples of Velazquez' famous pentimenti. The silhouette, the gesture, the grasp of the personage, and the composition are even more successful in the portrait of Olivares (Hispanic Society, New York), dating to 1625. Then, in the portrait of the Infante Don Carlos, the painter at one bound equaled the masters of aristocratic distinction in the male portrait—Titian, Van Dyck, the English. But there is no affectation in the elegance, it is compounded of nobility, ease, gravity, humanity, and also an indefinable natural grace. The model's inimitable way of holding his hat and dangling an empty glove from his finger-tips are two lucky finds. The invention goes well beyond realism or naturalism, it reveals the painter's determination to work out an unrhetorical style of his own.

Ochres now disappeared, and with his blacks Velazquez composed an orchestration of nuances such as only a great colorist is capable of. Though in the model's face linger traces of the strong plasticity of his Seville period, in the silhouette and play of values Velazquez has already met his problem: man in his surrounding atmosphere. Anecdote is absent; there is no furniture in the room, the figure stands alone, solitary as an apparition, like "something that looms into sight," as Ortega y Gasset aptly observed. Velazquez attenuated the outlines with a brush that freed the silhouette of any linear dryness. The model thus emerges enveloped in air, surrounded by a fluidity that moves with his figure and situates him in space. So it is that the references to a measured space are kept to a minimum. A mere brushstroke suffices to indicate the angle of intersection between floor and wall; later even this slight reference disappeared. Of this portrait, which already contains the whole of Velazquez, Beruete writes: "It is impossible to meet with a painting more alive, more perfect in its simplicity; nature is taken unawares by the synthetic vision of Velazquez and interpreted by him with innate superiority."

Thus the glory of the portraitist was already firmly established. But was Velazquez merely a portraitist? Nothing more than that, murmured the envious. The king resolved to put him to the test in a large composition. This was the *Expulsion of the Moriscoes* of 1627, now lost, which gave him his first chance of tackling a historical picture. Shortly afterwards he painted the *Triumph of Bacchus*, whose "logarithm of reality" found apt expression in its popular title: *The Topers*. Velazquez still stood in need of passive and patient sitters of character, such as would enable him to train his eye and pursue his investigation of life, for his brush remained obsessed, as it were, with the representation of life's irreducible singularities, as is proved by his first pictures of court jesters, which date from this period. *The Topers*, though it falls in line with his Sevillian works, denotes a higher ambition and raises a major problem: the anti-rhetorician Velazquez confronts mythology. He had already become acquainted with the great Italian masters, in the matchless

THE INFANTE DON CARLOS, 1625-1627. PRADO, MADRID.

gallery of the Alcazar in Madrid, and also with Rubens, but had remained virtually uninfluenced by them. His devotees of the cult of Bacchus might have stepped from the pages of *Lazarillo de Tormes* or *Guzman de Alfarache*, picaresque wine-bibbers grouped around a handsome, half-naked youth. This is prose without frivolity. *The Topers*, as Mayer has written, "have nothing in common with the coarse models used by Dutch painters." These are neither marionettes nor puppets; these are men. Once again appear the diagonal and the intersection of lines, the hands of light crowning the toper in the middle, and the eye can follow the path of light traced out by the arm of this prosaic Bacchus. But Velazquez has made a further discovery: landscape. A concrete, spacious, grandiose landscape, which spreads out from the banks of the Manzanares. But this was only a tentative effort; his greatest conquests in landscape came later, as his pictorial language was broadened and deepened, when he stood in full possession of his abbreviated manner and succeeded in making us feel atmosphere.

The destiny and fortune of Velazquez lay in the fact that, like Ribera, but with a vaster horizon, he was the only Spanish painter of his generation—the decisive generation of Spanish painting—who eluded isolation and provincialism. It was also his good fortune to enjoy the friendship of Rubens during the eight months the Flemish master spent in Madrid. Then there was his journey to Italy. This came as the complement of friendly relations maintained daily with the works of the great Italian masters in the Alcazar. Velazquez traveled to see and learn, and worked little abroad. But the two pictures he did paint in Rome owe something to Italy. His conception remains personal, and his differences from the Italian painters exceed his debt to them. In *Vulcan's Forge* Apollo informs Vulcan of the infidelity of Venus. There is no gesturing; the scandalous news makes the men pause in their work and centers their

JOSEPH'S COAT (DETAIL), 1630. PALACE OF THE ESCORIAL.

attention on the visitor. This restraint, charged with intensity, is the reverse of Caravaggio's frantic gesticulation, and equally far removed from the expressive urbanity of the Venetians or Guercino. More akin to the latter is *Joseph's Coat* (Escorial), although, as was the Spanish painter's way, the interest is again centered on the lozenge formed by the arms and hands of the two figures holding the bloodstained coat. The diagonal is

Vél. 15

—
⌐


THE TOPERS OR THE TRIUMPH OF BACCHUS, C. 1628.
PRADO, MADRID.

emphasized; planes of light and shadow divide the picture in a
carefully weighed proportion. The feeling for color and the
lighting are very different from Guercino's lunar clarity. Already,
behind the two figures coming up in the background, there
appears that screen of penumbra which Velazquez introduced
to mark his investigations of space. The glimpse of a landscape
denotes his awakening sense of a new vocation.

52

Another exceptional group of religious pictures dates from after his return from Italy in 1631. *Christ at the Column* (National Gallery, London) and *Christ on the Cross* (Prado) point to a growing interest in the nude which was certainly the result of this journey. But even in the most academic of his works, the London *Christ*, the pulse of life beats in the delightful figure of the little girl. The Prado *Christ* is an example of reserve and

JOSEPH'S COAT, 1630. PALACE OF THE ESCORIAL.

serenity rare in Christian iconography. This is a dead Christ depicted without emotionalism, at once real and distant. This painting inspired Unamuno to write a poem expressive of a profound religious sentiment aspiring to faith. The picture at Orihuela, the *Temptation of St Thomas Aquinas*, also has a fitness and restraint in contrast with the frenzied expression characteristic of his time. The composition rich in interior space, the variations of lighting, the still life elements, all are highly personal. As usual, the intense and sober expression is concentrated on the hands. Those of the angel are a matchless example of delicacy and sensibility.

This group of pictures, except for the Prado *Christ*, painted with bitumens which have sometimes led to the assumption that the work pre-dates his journey to Italy, vouches for the progress Velazquez was making in the handling of his medium. The palette is brighter and the execution freer, color being applied in light coats which, as with the Venetians, allow the grain of the canvas to show through. In the heads of the two pictures of *Vulcan's Forge* and *Joseph's Coat*, the simplification of technique, the scumbles and accents are a prodigy of accuracy. To fathom the secret of life Velazquez no longer needed to resort to the violent intensity of his Seville paintings; from now on his arms were lightness, allusiveness, economy of means. He was the contrary of a virtuoso.

# THE GLORIES OF BUEN RETIRO

A great task was waiting for Velazquez at the royal palace when he took up his brushes again after his return from Italy. In view of his unremitting, unerring investigation of life, it must have seemed as if he intended to reduce the whole of painting to the portrait of life. Weary of an idealized archetype, like that of Raphael or of Michelangelo, he felt within him the growing need to paint *individuals*. Now the artist hearkened to the call of things, he fell back on the poetry of life and discovered the mystery of unique experience, which can never repeat itself.

The trivial delineation of everyday life as we find it in the naturalism of the 19th century, in the so-called "nature piece," is something altogether different. With Velazquez, painting probed into one of the world's gravest mysteries—the mystery alluded to by philosophers when they speak of the *principium individuationis*. The naturalism of the 19th century was only a neo-style. Velazquez' realism is imbued with a will to transcendence. It answers to a Spanish vision of the world, aptly illustrated by the text of Fray Luis de Granada inscribed at the head of the second chapter of this volume. There is a book by Cardinal Bellarmine entitled *On the Knowledge of God through his Creatures*. This might be taken as the leitmotiv of Velazquez' art. To the Spanish mind, God resides not in the kind of intellectual club made up by the world of Platonic ideas, but reveals himself to us in the humblest realities. Human values derive from the mere fact of existing; and not from faith, duty, or the sense of a social mission, nor from intelligence or power.

At bottom, for a Spaniard, all men are truly equal, and it is for art to reflect this profound awareness of individualization, for the individual is transient and variable, as far as the matter goes of which he is made; but he is the truth as postulated for us not only by our intelligence but by our vital reason. Truth is existence and existence is history, and history too pursues truth. Cervantes has well expressed this in an often-quoted passage: "Because History is something sacred, it must be truthful; wheresoever is truth, there is God, truth being an aspect of the Godhead." To the humanist mind of the Renaissance, truth and art were opposed to each other. Velazquez set out in his painting to show the falsity of this alleged opposition. Lope de Vega agreed with him, and in his comedy *Lo fingido verdadero* he sums up his esthetic credo in these lines:

> "For those who cling to the rules of art
> Will never of true nature show any part."

Velazquez is the highest example of one of those moments, rarer than is commonly supposed in the history of art, which witness the triumph of what has been called in another field "the esthetic of the individual's salvation"; and this esthetic, in spite of momentary eclipses, was better suited than any other to the Spanish vocation in the great age of the 17th century. But let it not be forgotten that the Spaniard, being an extremist, is always ready to leap without transition to the opposite extreme. Witness Picasso and Miró, who in a way are no less Spanish than Velazquez.

Velazquez then lived through a few years of optimism at the Spanish court. A deceptive optimism it proved to be, a giddy sense of well-being trumped up and sustained by the dictator Olivares to flatter his monarch. And dictators, when they leave off telling their usual lies, either ignore or are blind to the truth. The favorite endeavored to create around his master

KING PHILIP IV ON HORSEBACK (DETAIL), C. 1636.
PRADO, MADRID.

THE SURRENDER OF BREDA OR THE LANCES, BEFORE 1635.
PRADO, MADRID.

an atmosphere of power and victory. The king spent his time
in an idle succession of hunting expeditions, country pleasures
and merry-making, performances of comedies and recitations
of poetry, love affairs with women of low birth, and the favorite
exploited the king's tendency to neglect the business of government. The palace of Buen Retiro with its architecture and its

gardens, due to the personal initiative of Olivares, remains the symbol of these years of counterfeit glory, when in reality the Spanish power lay on the brink of ruin and the empire was slowly falling apart. In 1631, at the first entertainment given at Buen Retiro, a comedy was performed with this symbolic title: "He who lies most will grow greatest." Here is a fitting motto for the dictatorships of all periods. In 1632 Olivares presented the king with the key to the new palace. The works to adorn it soon followed; he was then busying himself with the decoration of the main rooms. The heart of the palace was the so-called Salón de los Reinos. There, with a series of historical pictures, the minister planned to immortalize the victorious feats of arms which seemed to augur so well for the reign of Philip IV: victories won in the Low Countries, in Germany, in America, against the Dutch, against the coalitions at the start of the Thirty Years' War, against the English too. Velazquez was accordingly commissioned to represent the surrender of Breda, at the end of a long siege, during which the town was defended by Justin of Nassau, while the victorious army was led by the noble and accomplished Genoese general Ambrosio Spinola.

This is unquestionably the finest historical picture of European painting. Avoiding any suggestion of the rhetorical or pompous, Velazquez infused his work with his own courtesy and humanity. He represents, in the simplest way, the meeting of the two generals, at the moment the town capitulates. Spinola, an exemplary type of aristocratic amenity, bows with a smile toward his adversary and, with a scarcely perceptible gesture, spares him the humiliation of kneeling before the victor. Here are two antagonists who have played a fair game, and who may continue to be considered as two knights and gentlemen. A supreme lesson in good breeding and humanity which our time, with its pride in technical progress and science,

THE SURRENDER OF BREDA (DETAIL), BEFORE 1635.
PRADO, MADRID.

has forgotten. Velazquez composes his picture with flawless skill and great sobriety. The cross-pattern receding in depth in the form of an $X$ serves to focus attention on the central group, through a play of curves beginning in the foreground with the Dutch soldier seen from behind and the rump of the Spanish general's horse. The center of the picture and the

THE SURRENDER OF BREDA (DETAIL), BEFORE 1635.
PRADO, MADRID.

gist of its meaning are marked by Nassau's outstretched hand,
presenting the victor with the key to the city. A vast landscape
of flooded fields creates distance and atmosphere; the fires of
Breda cloud the horizon with smoke. Velazquez' palette is
richer and brighter than ever before; his composition is a find
full of happy invention. Obstinate investigators of sources and

influences have sought at all costs to point out antecedents of Velazquez' originality, but they cannot detract from his merit. Ortega y Gasset noted with his keen irony: "No sooner does a picture with a lance in the air turn up than we are asked to regard it as a precedent of the one by Velazquez. Looking closely at these precursors, it will be seen that much more genius would have been needed to dissociate this element of lances from their pictures and give it the role it plays in the *Surrender of Breda* than to invent everything *ex nihilo*." But unfortunately the specialists in art history, on the lookout for anything that will yield a magazine article or a paper for an art-historical congress, prefer to linger over the short-sighted, comparative analysis of photographs, instead of seeking to cultivate the enjoyment of works of art or to elicit their esthetic and historical significance.

*The Lances*, finished before 1635, stands out as the major achievement of this period. Yet his work as a portraitist is no less fine. The beautiful queen Isabelle de Bourbon did not like to pose, and this explains the mediocre quality of most of the portraits of her which have been preserved. Velazquez, passionately fond of the natural and vital, must have been able to do no more than lay in a few brushstrokes whenever the opportunity arose. To execute the large canvases ordered from him, he probably disposed only of a head painted from the model. Hence the suspicion that the extant portraits are only studio works. But two full-length portraits of the queen, with their fine colors, stand out from this middling production: one in Copenhagen Museum and another in an English collection. The pendant of this prototype may be the portrait of the king known as the *Silver Philip* in the National Gallery, London. What a distance separates this from the severe effigies of the previous decade! The dark dress and the ruff have been replaced by a rich costume which brings into play the full resources of

DON GASPAR DE GUZMAN, COUNT-DUKE OF OLIVARES, ON HORSEBACK (DETAIL),
C. 1638. PRADO, MADRID.

Velazquez' sumptuous palette, with its carmines beautifully setting off the king's golden hair, leather hat, gloves and plumes.

Large equestrian portraits of the royal family were ordered to embellish the palace of Buen Retiro. There are five of these. In three of them—those of Philip III, Queen Margarita, and Isabelle de Bourbon—Velazquez shared the work with others. The last-named portrait is a striking demonstration of the difference between Velazquez and his collaborators. The head of the queen and the horse are two superb pieces of painting, because here again Velazquez penetrated life, whereas those who painted the clothes and the backgrounds of the pictures were only mediocre imitators whose artless efforts were rendered insipid by their incapacity. Who were Velazquez' helpers? At that festive period the king's painter was surrounded by colleagues, painters of stage scenery, and decorators. Already collaborating with him was his faithful disciple and zealous imitator Juan Bautista del Mazo, who in 1634 had married his daughter Francisca. The two equestrian portraits entirely by the hand of Velazquez, that of Philip IV on a rearing horse and that of Prince Don Baltasar Carlos on his spirited young mare, are outstanding works, especially the latter, whose simplicity of execution is made surpassingly clear. Velazquez had been accustomed to painting the heir to the throne ever since the prince's earliest years (one of these childhood portraits is in Boston Museum). The lively trot of the horse seen from below, together with the beauty and finesse of the colors, and the superlative head of the boy prince, laid in with a light coat of paint that lends itself to masterly abbreviations and to smooth, shadowless modeling, all this constitutes a decisive landmark in the painter's work. And in these portraits of the child and his father, the landscapist in Velazquez has made marked progress in the representation of nature. What we have here are no longer, as has sometimes been said, mere

PRINCE DON BALTASAR CARLOS ON HORSEBACK, C. 1634.
PRADO, MADRID.

THE CARDINAL INFANTE DON FERNANDO OF AUSTRIA AS A HUNTER, 1632-1636.
PRADO, MADRID.

backdrops. We stand before carefully studied transcriptions of the panorama of Sierras and oak forests which surround Madrid, and in which, as Paul Claudel was to put it, "the mountains dance in a ring in chorus." The view corresponds to Velazquez' favorite lookout: the snowy peak in the distance, to the right of the prince's horse, is the Montaña de la Maliciosa in the central chain of the Sierra de Guadarrama.

The series of hunting portraits offers a new combination of the human figure and landscape. They were finished toward 1636, but the Infante Don Fernando, who is portrayed in one of them, had been absent from Madrid since 1632. So Velazquez must have painted his portrait from an earlier head study. The portrait of Prince Baltasar is a charming work. The posing, the naturalness and simplicity of these hunting portraits represent a step forward in the career of Velazquez and in his vocation as a landscape painter, for here he shows an amazing boldness of execution and a great freedom of touch. Velazquez has fully accepted animals, God's creatures, into his world. Seldom does an animal painter succeed in penetrating so deeply into the life-sources of noble animals.

Not many years were left to the Count-Duke to wield his power when Velazquez painted a portrait of him on horseback, probably in 1638. This, as Beruete said, is the very apotheosis of pride, that pride which grows inordinately in great ones as they approach their downfall. That of Olivares was now at hand. The Buen Retiro, whose decorations and entertainments were to remain as the symbol of a frivolous reign, had been his creation. In the ashes of remembrance, now that the palace has been destroyed and its masters have vanished from the earth, all that lives on for us are the music of Calderon's verses and a few paintings by Velazquez.

KING PHILIP IV AT FRAGA, 1644.
COPYRIGHT THE FRICK COLLECTION, NEW YORK.

# THE GRANDEUR AND MISERY OF MAN

> "A good portrait always appears to me like a dramatized biography, or rather like the natural drama inherent in every man."
>
> BAUDELAIRE, *1859 Salon.*

IN the decade beginning in 1640, the life of Velazquez, hitherto uneventful, entered on a more agitated phase. Events followed hard upon one another: the fall of Olivares, frequent journeys to accompany the king, the death of the young Prince Don Baltasar Carlos, heir to the throne, war and unrest in the kingdom, and finally a second journey to Italy.

There can be no question here of discussing all the paintings of Velazquez, but in order to understand the rich and complex texture of his production, it should be borne in mind that several parallel series of pictures developed at the same pace within the body of his work. Their chronology, never absolutely certain, and the advantage of considering these groups in their entirety allow us to single out at least the following series: religious paintings (*St Anthony Abbot and St Paul the Hermit* and the *Coronation of the Virgin*); mythological subjects, beginning with *Vulcan's Forge*; and portraits of court jesters.

Velazquez liked to seek relaxation from his official duties in painting the picaresque figures around him, dwarfs, court fools, and other hangers-on in the palace. This was not the first time in history that a king took pleasure in surrounding himself with such strange and miserable creatures; but the Baroque court of Philip IV was literally teeming with them. They came under all sorts of headings: professional jesters, dwarfs, harmless fools, freaks and degenerates. How else is this cortege of misery around the great of the earth to be accounted for, if not by the strange attraction exerted by the abnormal individuality making spectacularly evident the enigma of the *principium individuationis*?

THE DWARF DON DIEGO DE ACEDO, "EL PRIMO." ▶

THE DWARF DON SEBASTIAN DE MORRA. ▶

Here are the most famous portraits of court jesters and dwarfs which Velazquez painted. Each of these pictures testifies to his passion for representing the individual. Touched by the magic of a brush at once discreet and searching, even the most miserable creature assumes a moving dignity.

◄    THE COURT JESTER CALABACILLAS.

◄ FRANCISCO LEZCANO, "THE CHILD OF VALLECAS."

Presented together, in the order in which they figure on the walls of the Prado, these four portraits form an impressive "polyptych of freaks." They illustrate "the ills that flesh is heir to" and afford a cruel insight into the unconscious mind. Yet they inspire not repugnance but pity.

Velazquez could not fail to take an interest in this phenomenon, possessed as he was, ever since his youth, by what I have called the esthetic of the individual's salvation.

The bulk of these pictures of buffoons, with the exception perhaps of the *Geographer*, seem to have been painted after his return from Italy in 1631; entries in the palace archives, brought to light twenty years ago by Moreno Villa, bear this out. The full-length portrait of "Pablillos de Valladolid," of about 1632, is the first representation of a figure surrounded by space without any reference to perspective. Manet had it in mind when he painted *The Fifer*. "Don Juan of Austria," a wily buffoon who had derisively assumed the name of Philip II's glorious son, was painted about 1633, and "Barbarossa," a mad-cap swashbuckler, shortly after that date. The two pictures entitled *Aesop* and *Menippus* represent not actual court jesters, but two would-be philosophers. In the latter the dark tones appear to symbolize the servitudes of poverty, accepted however with an undaunted smile. The still life, which in the early works of Seville had such full-bodied volumes, is now reduced to shadowed planes which little by little lose their consistency and substance. In this delineation of the grandeur and misery of man, the four portraits painted by Velazquez of the court dwarfs represent the climax of a passionate investigation. A categorical warning against taking any pride in the human condition, this teratological repertory might be styled the "polyptych of freaks." The picture of the jester Calabacillas, sometimes mistakenly called the "idiot of Coria," no doubt begun before 1639 was later retouched; the three other dwarfs, El Primo, Don Sebastian de Morra, and Francisco Lezcano, the so-called "child of Vallecas," must have been painted at Saragossa in 1644. Working unhurriedly from these patient models, Velazquez abstracted himself from the harassing preoccupations that darkened the journey of the court.

These were bitter years for Spain: Portugal rebelled, the French invaded Catalonia, Olivares was dismissed, Sicily and Naples rose in arms, the nobles of Aragon and Andalusia conspired against the king, and the queen died, followed—fatal misfortune—by Baltasar Carlos, heir to the throne. Shortly before the prince's death, Velazquez had painted him in the picture in Vienna Museum, which is like the quintessence of the court portrait as he conceived it to be. The figure is seen full length, three-quarter face, or roughly so. The right arm is extended in a gesture expressing will and power, while the graceful curve of the left arm compensates for this authoritarian stiffness. The legs are firmly planted on the ground. Generally a red and gold upholstered armchair and a table spread with velvet make up a summary *mise en scène*. The background is divided into dark and light rectangles. Velazquez kept to a formula that had held good since the 16th century, and he was obliged to modify it scarcely at all in order to give it an archetypal value and to deepen the picture space. The portrait takes on an ambivalent, almost contradictory aspect: at once calm and dynamic in a composition of absolute clarity. The model's restful pose is charged with potential action. "Without any of the violence of a Tintoretto or a Daumier," writes Mayer, "these figures act like forces in space... Velazquez plumbs space in all directions."

When we extol the astonishing lifelikeness of these portraits by Velazquez, or the freedom of his technique made up of "distant spots" (as Quevedo described it) which anticipate Impressionism, it is well to remember that the first virtue of the painter lies in his total, unitary conception of the picture, in his construction in terms of forms. It is here that the artist shows his creative genius, and Velazquez does not fail to show his, although he does so with a discretion not always to be found in modern painters. Simplicity, measure, love of essentials, guide his brush. Mayer put it perfectly when he wrote, "What we admire above all in Velazquez is the instinctive sureness of his self-mastery. Everything in him is necessary: nothing is excessive, nothing is insufficient. From this results harmony in the attitude, in the composition, in the color scheme, in the expression." At a far remove from the view of Velazquez taken by the narrow-minded realists of the 19th century, Mayer draws all the inferences from this new comprehension: "The painting of Velazquez corresponds to the final form of the Greek vision of the natural, not in any outwardly naturalistic imitation, but in a simplifying realism which always ennobles nature, fortifies human qualities, and does away with the vulgarity of everything it touches. Without imitating the ancients, and even though setting himself in deliberate opposition to everything that goes by the name of the classical tradition, Velazquez, like Raphael before him, endows his creations with a clarity and self-evidence which in the end amounts to a kind of classicism." The Raphael of the Baroque age, such was Velazquez as seen by Mayer, and Beruete wrote that he was "more than a naturalist, because he did not content himself with reproducing a perishable form, but endeavored to penetrate its essence." Compare his portraits with those by other painters—Rubens, Van Dyck—of the same models: Philip IV, Isabelle de Bourbon, Don Fernando, Spinola. What for Velazquez is the essential dissolves in the others into mere lifelikeness and decorative adjuncts.

Velazquez was never so great a colorist as in the portrait of Philip IV in military costume (Frick Collection, New York) and in that of Pope Innocent X (Galleria Doria, Rome). The first was made in three sittings which the king granted his painter in the town of Fraga, in Aragon. The work was done in a makeshift studio fitted up on the spur of the moment, in a small room with shattered walls and no flooring, during a brief halt in the field in the course of the campaign of 1644.

PRINCE DON BALTASAR CARLOS, C. 1640.
KUNSTHISTORISCHES MUSEUM, VIENNA.

VIEW FROM THE VILLA MEDICI IN ROME  MIDDAY), 1650-1651.
PRADO, MADRID.

VIEW FROM THE VILLA MEDICI IN ROME (AFTERNOON), 1650-1651.
PRADO, MADRID.

POPE INNOCENT X, 1650.
GALLERIA DORIA-PAMPHILI, ROME.

In this bare room Velazquez worked as if he had been in a palace. This is perhaps the richest, most perfect portrait he ever made of his master. This harmony of pinks, blacks and silvery tints is one of the world's most exquisite, most sumptuous pieces of painting. His versatility enabled Velazquez to pass without any transition from this delightful work to the portraits of dwarfs, of which he seems to have painted at least three that same year, in the course of the same journey into Aragon. Under his profoundly human brush, these monsters inspire no feelings of repulsion. These pictures may be regarded as marking the climax of his passion for representing the individual. His love of life, which made him faithful to the mute exactitude of appearances, led him to plumb these unhappy creatures and to bring out, in their expression and gaze, the sediment common to us all, which gives to each existence a sufficient dignity. Incapable of lying, either before a king or before a buffoon, possessed by a need of transcendent truthfulness, he seems each time to be trying to understand his models with the best intentions of God.

This is the very attitude, ethically and esthetically unexceptionable, which Velazquez adopted toward the highest ranking personage who ever sat to him, Pope Innocent X. This unforgettable portrait is a monument of Western history. The pope cannot be said by any means to have an attractive face. This old Roman aristocrat of seventy-five, narrow-minded, with his grim, mistrustful glance, his thinning hair, his puffed and blotchy cheeks, was the least desirable of models for a painter of princes and grandees. Faithful to his implacable objectivity, the Spaniard made no effort to flatter so thankless a sitter, yet what dignity, what grandeur he gave him! Schopenhauer said that in front of this picture one has the impression of standing before a majesty of the earth. This impression springs from a purely esthetic quality: the monumentality which

84

POPE INNOCENT X (DETAIL), 1650. GALLERIA DORIA PAMPHILI, ROME.

Velazquez succeeded in imparting to the form, and which lies not in its size but in the expressive arrangement of lines and of the composition. So effective are the beautifully contrived accord of reds, whites and golds, and the abbreviated, synthetic execution of color patches, laid on in bold strokes, that this

◄ POPE INNOCENT X (DETAIL), 1650. GALLERIA DORIA PAMPHILI, ROME.

arresting portrait takes us by surprise even when we come to
analyze its smallest details. Looking at this painting, as at
those of princes and court jesters, we can say again with Justi
that Velazquez has painted "the tone of the nerves, the quality
of the vital sap, the proportion of iron and bile in the blood, of
prudence and folly in the brain." Nowhere else do we better
feel the truth of another of Justi's observations: "Compared
with that of Velazquez, Titian's coloring seems conventional,
Rembrandt's fantastic, and Rubens's affected with a certain
mannerism." For Sir Joshua Reynolds the portrait of Innocent X
was the "best painting in Rome," and this was the supreme
compliment in the mouth of the great English portraitist.

Rome also offered Velazquez an opportunity of giving us
an intimate testimony of his lyrical feeling for landscape: the
two small pictures showing views of the gardens of the Villa
Medici. In one the light of midday, in the other that of the
afternoon, in both a synthetic, allusive execution and an
exquisite sense of poetry, bring to mind, two centuries in
advance, the subtlest, most delicate notations of Corot.

At this same period, Velazquez, whose rare production
always offers facets of rich variety, also painted some masterly
portraits of children (the one owned by the Hispanic Society
of America, in New York, may be the artist's grand-daughter)
and of women. The *Lady with a Fan* (Wallace Collection,
London) is the most remarkable representation we have of the
Spanish woman in her gracious reserve. It is very possible
that this is Velazquez' daughter Francisca. A portrait of Archbishop Valdès is supposed to have turned up recently in an
English collection and Velazquez is known to have painted a
portrait of Cardinal Borgia which has been lost, but of which
some replicas remain, and above all an impressive chalk drawing
(Academy of San Fernando, Madrid), one of the few sure and
perfect examples of Velazquez' work as a draftsman.

THE LADY WITH A FAN, 1644-1648. REPRODUCED BY PERMISSION OF
THE TRUSTEES, WALLACE COLLECTION, LONDON.

To paint the grave and noble figure of a woman in the *Coronation of the Virgin* in the Prado, he had no need to depart very much from everyday humanity. In the same way, the two views of the Villa Medici simply voice, more intimately and personally, the serene and tender feeling for landscape which we find again in the picture of *St Anthony Abbot and St Paul the Hermit*, also in the Prado. Lastly, in the same vein of inspiration, there are the vast landscapes with hunting scenes, views of architecture, foliage in the gardens of Aranjuez, of which at least the delightful little figures owe something to the master's touch. This is a much disputed group of works, in which the participation of Mazo is generally recognized. It is impossible, however, to banish the idea that there is something of Velazquez' brush in these charming and masterly works.

# THE PARADOX OF REALITY

*"Just as Descartes reduces thought to rationality, so Velazquez reduces painting to visuality."*

JOSÉ ORTEGA Y GASSET.

PRESENT reality taken as the mainstay of the art of painting, this was the essential inspiration of Velazquez. But this inevitable presence, the prose and prop of our lives, has not, as might be imagined, merely a single significance. The plastic reality that Velazquez offers us in his early works is founded on what Berenson calls *tactile values*; in other words, on a semblance, intended to deceive the eye, of what we perceive through the sense of touch, of hardness, consistency, volumes, profiles. Starting out from this point, Velazquez proceeded to transform his painting by bending it to the evolution of his vision, which was ably served by an increasingly perfected technique. In time, more and more effectively, this initial reality was purged, synthesized, and finally overcome by the painter. Pure vision is the image, in an inaccessible space, that a mirror gives us. In a mirror, vision takes on the character of a concept: things are or are not, exist or vanish, just as to Calderon life appeared to be a dream, and dream life. Mirrors, as Pedro Penzol has pointed out, play an important role in several paintings by Velazquez. He was fond of them; in the inventory of his household belongings drawn up after his death, ten mirrors are listed. There comes to mind at once the picture in which a lovely Spanish woman, with slender waist and full hips, turns her back on us, out of disdain or coquetry. She chooses not to show her face, but equivocally reveals it to us in her looking glass, dim and ghostly. This is the Rokeby *Venus*. It is safe to say that this was neither the only Venus nor the only female nude Velazquez painted; but none other has come down to us. The prevailing opinion today is that the picture in the National Gallery of London was painted before 1651. A matchless color harmony tempers the warm Venetian tonality and Rubensian opulence with a graver, more Spanish accord of whites, leaden grays, blue and carmines, to which is added the brown ivory of the flesh tint. But most important of all here is the fact that the painter holds more aloof from appearances; his immediate perception of the tangible grows blurred; contours melt away and reality becomes more and more remote and paradoxical.

The mythological paintings in which, ever since his *Vulcan* and his *Mars*, Velazquez had been seeking atmospheric effects also lent themselves to this equivocal play, no doubt unconscious on the artist's part, and rather the fruit of intuition than of reasoning. Of the pictures on pagan themes which Velazquez painted for the Salón de los Espejos in the royal palace—mirrors again—in the last decade of his life, three perished in the terrible fire that ravaged the Alcazar in 1734; had it not been for this disaster, the Prado today would be richer to an even more fabulous degree than it is. All that now remains is the *Mercury and Argus*, painted about 1659, and it is a fine example of that almost bodiless painting to which the art of Velazquez attained in the end. This manner of painting, supremely light in texture, with a vagueness of outline which reduces bodies to an almost ghostly state, already appears in the "polyptych of freaks" and in the portrait of Pope Innocent X.

The main task that fell to Velazquez upon his return from Italy in 1651 was not too well suited to his bent toward this immaterial kind of painting, but he brought to bear on it the extreme subtlety of his technique. He had to paint portraits, a great many portraits, intended for very specific purposes: to immortalize, with force and distinction, first the king's new bride, the young Mariana of Austria, his niece, then the Infanta Maria Teresa, in whom the Habsburg features were enhanced

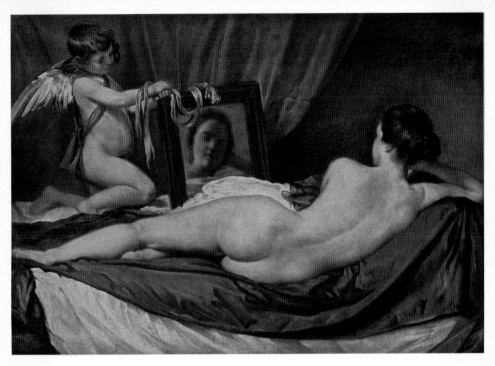

by those of her mother, Isabelle de Bourbon. Soon came the
children of Philip IV and Queen Mariana, the Infanta Margarita
and the Infante Felipe Prosper, heir to the throne, who died
however before he reached the age of three. The intensity of his
colors is greater than ever, and his palette brighter. Carmines,
silvery tints and vermilions form, as it were, a crescendo in the
great fugue of Velazquez' final style. It is as if the painter,
having deepened his insight into his models, were drawing from

THE INFANTA MARIA TERESA, 1653. KUNSTHISTORISCHES MUSEUM, VIENNA.

them a more intense and at the same time more intimate note, especially in the portraits of children, who always so much appealed to him and quickened his inspiration. His technique, more and more abbreviated as time went on, reduced tactile values to chromatic allusions.

A study of these portraits shows the rich gamut of harmonies then dominant in the painter's palette. Mariana of Austria, like a royal doll, rouged and powdered, has a majestic and solemn air in spite of her monstrous gown, whose black velvet sets off the silver trimmings. Against this sober color scheme rings out the rich note struck by carmines, vermilions and golds. A haughty idol, such is the new queen, niece and wife of Philip IV, who had once entertained hopes of marrying her to his son, the ill-starred prince Baltasar Carlos.

Like Goya, Velazquez had the knack of adapting himself to his models and swathing them in an orchestration of colors inspired by their character and physiognomy. He set out to make no display of psychology, but instinctively chose from his palette the harmony of tones best suited to the person portrayed, brought out with convincing elegance his or her personality, and surrounded it with a well-defined spiritual atmosphere whose undertones he skillfully varied according to the model's particular character.

The series of family portraits sent to the court at Vienna, and unusually well preserved in the great museum of the old Imperial city, offers a perfect example of this skill and exquisite taste. In order to grasp clearly the two poles of the art of Velazquez, whose esthetic embraced human grandeur as well as human misery, we can do no better than compare what we have called the "polyptych of freaks" with a parallel series of paintings, that polyptych of beauty and grace on the walls of Vienna Museum. It was the good fortune of the Imperial court to receive, in pictures by Velazquez, the most delightful

THE INFANTA MARGARITA, C. 1656.
KUNSTHISTORISCHES MUSEUM, VIENNA.

THE INFANTA MARGARITA IN A BLUE GOWN, C. 1659.
KUNSTHISTORISCHES MUSEUM, VIENNA.

embassy possible. The Infanta Maria Teresa, daughter of Isabelle de Bourbon, was the loveliest feminine ornament of the court of Madrid, and her future marriage was one of the cornerstones of Spanish foreign policy; with the Rokeby *Venus* and the *Lady with a Fan*, she deserves to figure in any anthology of the most beautiful women painted by Velazquez. To bring out her distinction and youth with sobriety, he chose silvery accents—her jewels and handkerchief—and lines lightly underscored with rosy carmine—her neck, arms and headdress. And to make the bright and luminous richness of her person stand out better, he surrounded it with velvety green.

It is this unostentatious distinction that makes Velazquez' paintings appear of so manifest an excellence and simplicity, a simplicity that seems to raise no problems. His style resides precisely in this sobriety, which may be called classical. But when we approach the picture for a look at the details, everything vibrates, grows indistinct, and scintillates in the isolated dabs of each brushstroke. The painter's analysis of his model consists in breaking it down into purposeful color patches charged with a synthetic power which already allows for the fusion of these separate touches when seen at a distance. The spirited lightness of his brush is best exemplified in jewels, plumes and hair which, when seen at close range, appear to be so many shapeless dabs of paint. The enchantment of childhood is conveyed in the supreme refinement of colors which seem predestined to express tenderness. Such is the portrait of the Infanta Margarita with a vase of flowers, of about 1653, also in Vienna Museum. The rose that has fallen from the vase (reproduced in detail on the title page) is, in its pictorial execution, a piece of pure abstraction such as a present-day painter might have produced. A silvery gray sings out alongside golds and reds in the later portrait of the Infanta Margarita, made about 1656, which served as a study for *Las Meninas*.

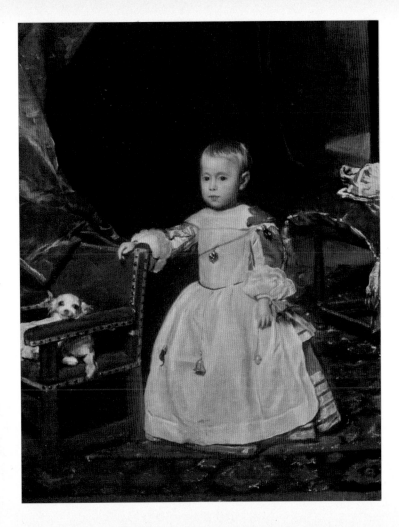

PRINCE FELIPE PROSPER, 1659. KUNSTHISTORISCHES MUSEUM, VIENNA.

PRINCE FELIPE PROSPER, DETAIL: THE DOG, 1659.
KUNSTHISTORISCHES MUSEUM, VIENNA.

The position of the arms accentuates the triangular composition of the silhouette founded on the hoop skirt, whose awkward, bulky framework thus fits smoothly into the picture pattern and color scheme invented by the painter.

Some three years later, in 1659, again for the court of Vienna, he painted the portrait of the short-lived heir to the Spanish throne, born of the king's second marriage, Prince Felipe Prosper. In this, perhaps the finest portrait of a child in all European painting, Velazquez, as in his portrait of Innocent X, sought to pay to his future Catholic Majesty— doomed in this case to an early death—the sumptuous homage of color. The problems of space receding in depth and the rich furnishings of chairs, curtains and rugs contribute to present the figure of the royal child with supreme, almost miraculous simplicity; and answering to the child, in a kind of sprightly counterpoint, is the little white dog silhouetted against the deep red velvet of the miniature armchair. The lightness of the texture, the scumbles as subtle as in a water-color, the color scheme of silver gray and pink, are all remarkable. And Velazquez painted the dog with no less loving care than the child. His human sympathy went in equal measure to all God's creatures.

In this same year, 1659, he was again called on to paint the Infanta Margarita who, though only eight years old, became a candidate for an imperial betrothal, now that the marriage of her sister Maria Teresa with Louis XIV of France had been decided on. Though still so young, she had to be represented —and this was the purpose of the portrait—with a royal dignity symbolizing her future destiny. A blue farthingale trimmed with gold and silver, the rich texture of her fur muff, and the dark, noble reflections of furniture in the background give this work a severer harmony than in the previous portraits of the Infanta. The child appears about to hold an audience.

THE INFANTA MARGARITA IN A BLUE GOWN (DETAIL), C. 1659.
KUNSTHISTORISCHES MUSEUM, VIENNA.

There is perhaps an even greater boldness in the execution
and details, and passages might be singled out so rich and
full-bodied in color, so free in form and handling, that they
surpass the most inspired painting of the best abstract *tachiste*
of the present day. The exquisite lavishness of the texture, the
nervous, life-enhancing vibrancy, and the incredible lightness

THE INFANTA MARGARITA IN A BLUE GOWN (DETAIL), C. 1659.
KUNSTHISTORISCHES MUSEUM, VIENNA.

of touch make these fragments so many anthology pieces
heralding the finest discoveries of the modern sensibility and
confirming the truth of Justi's comment: "It is as if he set out
to demonstrate that poetry can be extracted from prose and...
the fanciful from the natural." Remember too the question
which, well in advance of his time, the great German critic

asked himself in front of other pictures by the Spanish master: "Could it be that in art the object is nothing and the language everything?" This question points the way to the modern esthetic. It raises the problem of the liberties taken by the painter in his interpretation. And with this consideration El Greco, Velazquez, Goya, and the boldest of contemporary painters are seen to fall in line with each other.

The "brutal sketches" for which Pacheco had condemned El Greco appeared now in the work of Velazquez, but with him they served another purpose. It is only by isolating and enlarging particular details, which photography today makes easy, that we can be brought to realize how very far Velazquez was carried by his revolutionary attitude. His great simplicity and his sober, refined taste in the presentation of the figure now bore their final fruit, for example in the half-length portrait of Philip IV in the Prado. This intimate effigy of the king, a sadder and wiser man, awaking to the consciousness of his wasted life, is indeed the last picture that the visitor to the Prado should see, in his pilgrimage to the sanctuary of Velazquez' art. Lefort has described the impression it made on him: "This painting makes all its formidable neighbors seem to us like set images, lifeless or conventional: Van Dyck heavy, Rubens stodgy, and Tintoretto sallow; Velazquez alone gives us, in all its plenitude, the illusion of life." Yes, and how far he is already from Caravaggio and Caravaggism! Consider the head of this king and you will agree with Ruskin, even though his choice of names may seem to you too arbitrary or personal, that if we merely want to count the hairs on a head, a poster painter or an anatomist will do very well, but to represent the few that are visible is a matter only for the supreme masters, Carpaccio, Tintoretto, Reynolds or Velazquez.

We now know, as a result of the research work of the last few years, that the famous picture always called *Las Hilanderas*

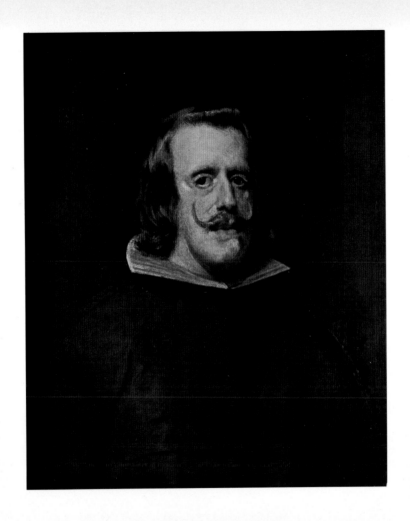

PORTRAIT OF PHILIP IV, 1655-1659.
PRADO, MADRID.

THE TAPESTRY WEAVERS ("LAS HILANDERAS"), 1657-1660. PRADO, MADRID.

(the *Spinners* or *Tapestry Weavers*), in the Prado, actually represents a mythological theme: Pallas and Arachne. Velazquez is true to his methods; he reduces the fantastic to an allusion, and he withdraws and attenuates the anecdote. The story unfolds only on the tapestry hanging in the background. As in his early work, *Christ in the House of Martha*, everyday reality occupies the foreground, here in the guise of a tapestry workshop.

THE TAPESTRY WEAVERS (DETAIL), 1657-1660. PRADO, MADRID.

THE TAPESTRY WEAVERS (DETAIL), 1657-1660. PRADO, MADRID.

THE TAPESTRY WEAVERS (DETAIL), 1657-1660. PRADO, MADRID.

The true subject is the light that plays over bodies and makes them unreal, haloing the background figures with its strongest beams or reducing them to a curtain of indistinct forms melting into the penumbra. By setting the subject in a tapestry workshop, Velazquez found for it the logarithm of reality defined by Ortega, and Americo Castro considers that the mythological theme is no more important in the picture than the fact of having embodied the abstract figures of the fable in Spanish women spinning and threading yarn and in aristocratic ladies looking at the tapestry. But, most important of all, these figures are reduced pictorially to pure color values, to forms dissolved in light, to "distant patches," to a transfigured reality. The great writer Quevedo, a contemporary of the artist, dedicated these lines to him, in which, in his Baroque style, he expressed already these very ideas:

> "From the light support of the painting,
> the color flees like shadow,
> denying the relief the hand would find."

The picture of the *Tapestry Weavers* does not belie this poetic interpretation; on the contrary, it shows us how Velazquez' method and his vision of nature have accentuated his highly personal procedure of eliminating plastic modeling, or rather of reducing it to pure color values, to almost flat forms floating in light and space. The painting thus becomes pure appearance, pure visuality, reality subjectivated to the extreme limit, to the point where it seems about to vanish. This is the paradox of reality admitted only in so far as it constitutes a presence for us. Searching out the basis of truth, which would enable him to construct the world intellectually, Descartes arrived at the formula "I think, therefore I am." The sole basis of existence is in the thought, the awareness, that each man has of himself. Pursuing the parallel so acutely emphasized by Ortega y Gasset, I might say that for Velazquez, from the painter's visual point

THE MAIDS OF HONOR ("LAS MENINAS"), 1656. PRADO, MADRID.

of view, real existence has as its sole basis the pure appearance that one finds in oneself and the pure color values in which lines, volume, bodies, and tactile values are diluted. The thing pictured becomes the ghost of itself. The purpose of the *Tapestry Weavers*, as of the *Maids of Honor*, is to give a definitive formulation of this pictorial testament of Velazquez.

THE MAIDS OF HONOR (DETAIL), 1656. PRADO, MADRID.

THE MAIDS OF HONOR (DETAIL), 1656. PRADO, MADRID.

If we can speak of impressionism in connection with Velazquez, this, as Oskar Hagen has noted, is because he succeeded in representing things just as they appear, as a shapeless aggregate of colored planes. The volumes of his early paintings, with their hard, polished contours, have become apparitions no less ghostly for being real or present to us. In the *Maids of Honor*, the Baroque painting *par excellence*, where is the picture, where is the reality? Already Velazquez was playing with paradoxical ambivalence. We are told that the artist has portrayed himself in the act of painting the royal couple, dimly visible in a mirror at the back of the room. But what is offered us is the group of bystanders watching the royal couple pose: the little Infanta, her maids of honor and retinue gathered around her. The subject of the picture is not on the canvas but in the space where the beholder stands. The figures themselves are looking at what is presumably the subject, whose place we ourselves occupy as we look at them. Under the play of lights and shadows, forms melt away. The focal unity of the picture is centered on the blond hair of the Infanta; from this point, everything runs off like the notes of a fugue and loses every value save its pure relation to the other notes. The brooch on the Infanta's breast, her little hand resting on her hoop skirt, the bright gleams in the women's hair and on the silk of their gowns, the large head and coarse features of the dwarf, the spectral shadows of the steward and the duenna—in all this there is nothing now but vague forms in process of dissolution. But then, to bring us back to reality, there is the artist himself who seems to be painting us; and to prove to us that light alone gives existence to form, there, at the farthest point from the eye, is the open door, with sunlight pouring in from behind and the courtier pausing on the steps, who serves as a screen and gives an idea of the distances in the room. The fact is that the picture has a tightly knit structure; a scaffolding of straight lines stands out strongly; this is a "small castle of rectangles," as Penzol put it. These rectangles, alleges my friend the Spanish architect Luis Moya, correspond in their relationships to the golden section; but another great Spanish writer, Buero Vallejo, who is also a painter, has convinced me in a private conversation that the perspective of *Las Meninas* cannot be resolved geometrically! Pure visuality, pure appearance—this paradoxical reality defies commentary.

THE MAIDS OF HONOR (DETAIL), 1656. PRADO, MADRID.

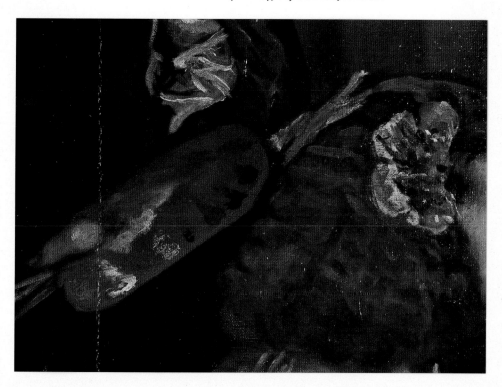

And this is why it could be so often repeated that the ultimate secret of a great work of art remains forever impenetrable.

Classical or Renaissance art constructs its ideal types and fixes its canons of beauty by abstracting certain elements from reality: line, form, design, mathematical or rational space, and what Leonardo called "universal light." The nominalist art of Velazquez falls back on the world of man, on the everyday world, on visual appearances, thanks to which things overflow their outlines and reduce the entity of volumes to pure color patches, and space to atmospheric values. But with the visual sincerity of his subjective picture order, Velazquez perceives and reflects the instantaneity of a single moment, which can never repeat itself. He sought to record time in the spatial vision that painting offers us, thereby enabling us to salvage something of passing time. The classical masters aspired to perpetuate ideas, symbols of perfect but timeless beauties. Velazquez aspired to immortalize man in the flesh, and to capture the poetry of the fleeting instant. This lyrical, suggestive manner of responding to the mystery of existence is what makes him the first modern painter.

SELECTED BIBLIOGRAPHY

INDEX OF NAMES AND PLACES

TABLE OF CONTENTS

# SELECTED BIBLIOGRAPHY

## General Works

P. DE MADRAZO, *Catálogo descriptivo e histórico del Museo del Prado*, Madrid 1872. — P. DE MADRAZO, *Viaje artístico de tres siglos*, Barcelona 1884. — J. R. MÉLIDA, *Bibliografía de Velázquez*, Revista de Archivos, Bibliotecas y Museos, Madrid 1899. — A. M. DE BARCIA, *Catálogo de la Colección de dibujos originales de la Biblioteca Nacional*, Madrid 1906. — A. DE BERUETE Jr., *The School of Madrid*, London 1909. — A. L. MAYER, *Die Sevillaner Malerschule*, Leipzig 1911. — P. BEROQUI, *Adiciones al Catálogo del Museo del Prado*, Boletín de la Sociedad Castellana de Excursiones, 1914-1915. — N. SENTENACH, *Los grandes retratistas de España*, Madrid 1914. — J. ALLENDE SALAZAR and F. J. SÁNCHEZ CANTÓN, *Retratos del Museo del Prado*, Madrid 1919. — A. L. MAYER, *Geschichte der Spanischen Malerei*, 2nd edition, Leipzig 1922 (in Spanish, 1st edition, 1928, 2nd edition, 1942). — V. VON LOGA, *Die Malerei in Spanien*, Berlin 1923. — F. J. SÁNCHEZ CANTÓN, *Dibujos españoles*, Madrid 1930. — E. LAFUENTE FERRARI, *La pintura española del siglo XVII*, Historia del Arte Labor, Vol. XII, Barcelona 1935 (2nd edition, 1945). — E. DABIT, *Les maîtres de la peinture espagnole, le Greco, Vélasquez*, Paris 1937. — Jacques LASSAIGNE, *Spanish Painting*, Geneva 1951. — E. LAFUENTE FERRARI, *Breve Historia de la Pintura Española*, 4th edition, Madrid 1953.

## Documents

M. R. ZARCO DEL VALLE, *Documentos inéditos para la historia de las bellas artes en España*, Vol. 55 of the *Colección de documentos inéditos para la Historia de España*, Madrid 1870. — P. DE MADRAZO, *Discurso de ingreso en la Real Academia de Bellas Artes de San Fernando*, Madrid 1870. — G. CRUZADA VILLAAMIL, *Informaciones de Velázquez para el ingreso en la Orden de Santiago*, Revista Europea, Madrid 1874. — Marquis de LAURENCIN, *Nuevos documentos*, Revista de Archivos, 1902. — J. R. MÉLIDA, *Un recibo de Velázquez*, Revista de Archivos, 1904. — PÉREZ PASTOR, *Noticias y documentos relativos a la Historia y a la Literatura española*, Madrid 1914. — F. J. SÁNCHEZ CANTÓN, *Los pintores de cámara de los reyes de España*, Madrid 1917. — *Documentos para la historia del arte en Andalucía*, Laboratorio de Arte de Sevilla, 1927-1946. — C. LÓPEZ MARTÍNEZ, *Arquitectos, escultores y pintores vecinos de Sevilla*, Seville 1928. — C. LÓPEZ MARTÍNEZ, *De Martínez Montañés a Pedro Roldán*, Seville 1932. — M. HERRERO GARCÍA, *Un dictamen pericial de Velázquez...*, Revista española de arte, 1936. — E. LAFUENTE FERRARI, *La inspección de los retratos reales en el signo XVII* (with an autograph of Velazquez), Correo Erudito, 1942. — F. J. SÁNCHEZ CANTÓN, *Cómo vivía Velázquez*, Madrid 1942.

## Literary Sources

Vicente CARDUCHO, *Diálogos de la Pintura*, Madrid 1633. — Francisco PACHECO, *Arte de la Pintura*, Seville 1649 (new edition by G. CRUZADA VILLAAMIL, 1866, and by F. J. SÁNCHEZ CANTÓN, Madrid 1956). — Jusepe MARTÍNEZ, *Discursos practicables del nobilísimo arte de la pintura*, edited by Valentin Carderera, Madrid 1866. — Antonio PALOMINO DE CASTRO Y VELASCO, *El Museo pictórico y escala óptica*, Madrid 1715-1724 (the life of Velazquez contained in Part III was reprinted in *Fuentes literarias para la historia del arte español*, published by F. J. SÁNCHEZ CANTÓN, Vol. IV; also consult the text by DIAZ DEL VALLE in the same publication). — Marco BOSCHINI, *L'arte del navegar pitoresco*, Venice 1660.

## Monographs

W. STIRLING, *Velazquez and his Works*, London 1855. — W. THORÉ BÜRGER, *Trésors d'art en Angleterre*, Brussels 1860. — W. STIRLING, *Essay towards a Catalogue of Prints engraved from the Works of Velazquez*, London 1873. — Charles Berwick CURTIS, *Velásquez and Murillo. A Descriptive Catalogue*, London-New York 1883. — G. CRUZADA VILLAAMIL, *Anales de la vida y obra de Diego Velázquez de Silva*, Madrid 1885. — P. A. LEFORT, *Vélasquez*, Paris 1888. — K. JUSTI, *Velazquez und sein Jahrhundert*, Bonn 1888 (1927, 1933; English edition, *Velazquez and his Times*, London 1889; Spanish edition, 1953). — W. ARMSTRONG, *Velazquez*, London 1895. — A. DE BERUETE, *Velazquez*, Paris 1898 (in English, 1906; in German, 1909). — Mesonero ROMANOS, *Velázquez fuera del Museo del Prado*, Madrid 1899. — J. Octavio PICÓN, *Vida y obras de don Diego Velázquez*, Madrid 1899. — Elie FAURE, *Vélasquez*, Paris 1903. — H. KNACKFUSS, *Velazquez*, Leipzig 1905. — Auguste BRÉAL, *Velazquez*, London 1905, Paris 1919. — Paul LAFOND, *Diego Vélasquez*, Paris 1906. — H. VOLLMEHR, article on Velazquez in Thieme-Becker, *Allgemeines Lexikon* (large bibliography), Leipzig 1907 et seq. — A. DE BERUETE, *El Velázquez de Parma*, Madrid 1911. — A. L. MAYER, *Kleine Velazquez-Studien*, Munich 1913. — AMAN-JEAN, *Vélasquez*, Paris 1913. — A. DE BERUETE Jr., *Velázquez en el Museo del Prado*, Madrid 1914. — J. MORENO VILLA, *Velázquez*, Madrid 1920. — A. DE BERUETE Jr. *La paleta de Velázquez*, Madrid 1922. — A. L. MAYER, *Velazquez*, Berlin 1924. — J. ALLENDE SALAZAR, *Velazquez*, Klassiker der Kunst, 4th edition, Stuttgart 1925 (the earlier editions were by W. GENSEL and V. VON LOGA). — G. ROUCHÈS, *Vélasquez*, Paris 1935. — A. L. MAYER, *Velazquez*, *A Catalogue Raisonné of the Pictures and Drawings*, London 1936. — E. TORMO, *Un resumen de Velázquez* (publication in Spanish of the author's article on Velazquez in the Enciclopedia Italiana), Boletín de la Sociedad Española de Excursiones, 1941. — A. L. MAYER, *Vélasquez*, Paris 1941. — A. MUÑOZ, *Velazquez*, Rome 1941. — E. LAFUENTE FERRARI, *Velazquez, Introduction and Catalogue*, London 1943. — F. J. SÁNCHEZ CANTÓN, *Las Meninas y sus personajes*, Barcelona 1943. — Neil MacLAREN, *The Rokeby Venus*, London n.d. — E. Lafuente Ferrari, *Velázquez*, Barcelona 1944. — Juan de la Encina (Ricardo Gutierrez Abascal), *Velázquez*, Mexico City 1944. — Léon-Paul Fargue, *Vélasquez*, Paris 1946. — Rafael Benet, *Velazquez*, Barcelona 1946. — Bernardino de Pantorba (José López Jiménez), *Velázquez*, Madrid 1946. — D. Angulo Iñiguez, *Velázquez. Como compuso sus principales cuadros*, Madrid 1947. — Elizabeth du Gué Trapier, *Vélasquez*, Paris 1948. — Carlos Flexa Ribeiro, *Velázquez e o realismo*, Rio de Janeiro 1949. — José Ortega y Gasset, *Papeles sobre Velázquez y Goya*, Madrid 1951. — José Ortega y Gasset, *Velazquez*, Zurich 1953.

## Magazine Articles

Adolfo Venturi, *Velazquez e Francesco I d'Este*, Nuova Antologia, 1881. — Emile Michel, *Diego Velázquez*, La España Moderna, 1894. — A. M. Barcia Pabon, *Velázquez en la Sección de Estampas de la Biblioteca Nacional*, Revista de Archivos, Bibliotecas y Museos, Madrid 1899. — J. R. Mélida, *Los Velázquez de la Casa de Villahermosa*, Revista de Archivos, 1905. — N. Sentenach, *Las Lanzas y las Hilanderas*, Boletín de la Sociedad Española de Excursiones, 1906. — A. de Beruete, *Velázquez y Gainsborough*, Ateneo, 1906. — Sir Charles Robinson, *The Bodegones and Early Works of Velazquez*, Burlington Magazine, 1906-1907. — A. de Beruete, *La Venus del Espejo*, Cultura Española, 1906. — V. von Loga, *Hat Velazquez radiert?*, Jahrbuch der preuss. Kunstsammlungen, Berlin 1908. — V. von Loga, *Las Meninas*, Jahrbuch der kunsthistorischen Sammlungen, Vienna 1909. — Roger Fry, *The Fraga Velazquez*, Burlington Magazine, 1911. — E. Tormo, *Velázquez y el Salón de Reinos*, Boletín de la Sociedad Española de Excursiones, 1912. — V. von Loga, *Estudios velazquistas*, Boletín de la Sociedad Española de Excursiones, 1914. — A. L. Mayer, *Über einige Velazquez zu unrecht zugeschriebene Stilleben und Genrebilder*, Monatshefte für Kunstwissenschaft, 1915. — Rafael Domenech Gallissá, *Velazquez y el impresionismo de la forma*, Boletín de la Sociedad Española de Excursiones, 1915. — Manuel Gómez Moreno, *El Cristo de San Plácido*, Boletín de la Sociedad Española de Excursiones, 1916. — A. de Beruete Jr., *Vélasquez ou Mazo?*, Gazette des Beaux-Arts, 1917. — M. de Villaurrutia, *El Papa de Velázquez*, Arte Español, 1920. — Walter W. S. Cook, *Spanish and French Paintings in the Lehman Collection*, Art Bulletin, 1924. — L. Justi, *Die Landschaften des Velazquez*, Repertorium für Kunstwissenschaft, 1927. — Franz Wolter, *Der junge Velazquez*, Munich 1929. — Tancred Borenius, *Velazquez's Portrait of Gongora*, Burlington Magazine, 1931. — H. Voss, *Zur Kritik des Velazquez Werkes*, Jahrbuch des preuss. Kunstsammlungen, Berlin 1932. — E. Lafuente Ferrari, *En torno a Velázquez*, Archivo Español de Arte y Arqueología, 1932. — Christopher Norris, *Velazquez and Tintoretto*, Burlington Magazine, 1932. — A. L. Mayer, *Problemas velazqueños*, Revista Española de Arte, 1933. — L. Zahn, *Callot und Velazquez*, Die graphische Künste, 1936. — Francis Howard,

*The Silver Philip*, Connoisseur, 1937. — F. J. Sánchez Cantón, *La libreria de Velazquez*, Archivo Español de Arte, 1942. — Marquis de Saltillo, *En torno a las Meninas y sus personajes*, Arte Español, 1944. — F. J. Sánchez Cantón, *New Facts about Velázquez*, Burlington Magazine, 1945. — Walter W. S. Cook, *Spanish Paintings in the National Gallery of Art*, Gazette des Beaux-Arts, 1945. — J. López Rey, *On Velazquez's Portrait of Cardinal Borja*, Art Bulletin, 1946. — D. Angulo Iñiguez, *Las Hilanderas*, Archivo Español de Arte, 1948. — Hans Soehner, *El estado actual de la investigación sobre Velázquez*, Clavileño, 1951. — Everett W. Hesse, *Calderón y Velázquez*, Clavileño, 1951. — J. M. Pita Andrade, *Los cuadros de Velázquez y Mazo que poseyó el Marqués del Carpio*, Archivo Español de Arte, 1952. — Pedro Penzol, *Los espejos en Velázquez*, Clavileño, 1952. — Martin S. Soria, *La Venus, los Borrachos y la Coronación de Velázquez*, Archivo Español de Arte, 1953. — Martin S. Soria, *Las Lanzas y los retratos ecuestres de Velázquez*, Archivo Español de Arte, 1954. — J. J. Martín González, *Sobre las relaciones entre Nardi, Carducho y Velázquez*, Archivo Español de Arte, 1958. — José López Rey, *A Pseudo Velazquez*, Gazette des Beaux-Arts, 1959.

# INDEX OF NAMES AND PLACES

TINTORETTO (1518-1594) 13, 18, 21, 28, 77, 102;
Venice, Ducal Palace: *Allegory of the Glory* (sketch in the Prado) 18.
TITIAN (1477?-1576) 18, 21, 28, 47, 86.
Toledo 5, 27, 32.
Thirty Years' War 59.
Trent 17.

UCEDA Juan de, painter 7.
UNAMUNO Miguel de (1864-1936) 45, 54.

Valencia 5.
Valsain woods 21.
Vatican 13.

VELAZQUEZ Diego (1599-1660), works mentioned:

Berlin Museum: *Musical Trio* (c. 1618) 34, 35;

Boston, Museum of Fine Arts: *Prince Baltasar Carlos with his Dwarf* (c. 1631) 64; *Portrait of Gongora* (1622) 9, 43, 46;

Budapest Museum: *Peasants at Table* (c. 1617) 34;

Chicago, Art Institute: *The Servant* (c. 1619) 34; *St John the Baptist* (c. 1620) 38;

Copenhagen, Royal Museum: *Isabelle de Bourbon* (c. 1636) 62;

Edinburgh, National Gallery: *The Old Cook* (1617-22) 31, 35, 36;

England, Private Collections: *Archbishop Valdès* (c. 1643) 86; *Isabelle de Bourbon* (c. 1636) 62;

Escorial, Salas Capitulares: *Joseph's Coat* (1630) 51/54;

Havana, Oscar B. Cintas Collection: *The Vintager*, attribution (c. 1618) 34;

Leningrad, Hermitage: *Peasants at Table* (c. 1617) 34;

London, National Gallery: *Christ in the House of Martha* (1617-19) 35, 39, 104; *Christ at the Column* (1631-32) 53; *Portrait of Philip IV* (*Silver Philip*, c. 1632-34) 62; *Rokeby Venus* (1648/51) 89, 91, 93;

London, Apsley House, Wellington Museum: *Two Young Men at Table* (c. 1618) 34; *The Water Carrier of Seville* (1618-20) 33, 37, 38;

London, Sir Alfred Beit Collection: *The Servant* (c. 1619) 34, 35;

London, Laurie Frere Estate: *Immaculate Virgin* (c. 1619) 38;

London, Wallace Collection: *Lady with a Fan* (1644-48) 86, 87, 93;

Longford Castle, Salisbury, Earl of Radnor: *Portrait of Juan de Pareja* (1649) 19;

Madrid, Academy of San Fernando: *Cardinal Borgia* (chalk drawing, c. 1643) 12, 86;

Madrid, Biblioteca Nacional: *View of Granada* (sepia drawing, 1648) 15;

Madrid, Prado:
Religious Pictures: *Adoration of the Magi* (1619) 40; *Coronation of the Virgin* (1641-43) 69, 88; *Christ on the Cross* (1631-32) 53, 54; *St Anthony Abbot and St Paul the Hermit* (1641-43) 69, 88;
Mythological Scenes: *Mars* (1640-42) 90; *Mercury and Argus* (c. 1659) 90; *Triumph of Bacchus* (*The Topers*, c. 1628) 13, 48, 50, 52; *Vulcan's Forge* (1630) 50, 54, 69, 90;

Landscapes: *View from the Villa Medici in Rome (Midday)* (1650-51) 80, 86, 88; *View from the Villa Medici in Rome (Afternoon)* (1650-51) 81, 86, 88;

Buffoons, dwarfs, etc.: *Aesop* (c. 1638) 76; *Barbarroja (Barbarossa)* (after 1633) 76; *Calabacillas ("The Idiot of Coria"*, before 1639) 71, 76; *Don Diego de Acedo ("El Primo")* (1644) 73, 76; *"Don Juan of Austria"* (c. 1633) 76; *Francisco Lezcano ("The Child of Vallecas")* (c. 1644) 72, 76; *Menippus* (c. 1638) 76; *Pablillos de Valladolid* (c. 1632) 76; *Don Sebastian de Morra* (1643-44) 74, 76;

Portraits: *Prince Baltasar Carlos on Horseback* (c. 1634) 64, 65, 67; *Prince Baltasar Carlos as a Hunter* (c. 1636) 67; *Infante Don Carlos* (1625-27) 47, 49; *Cardinal-Infante Don Fernando of Austria as a Hunter* (1632-36) 66, 67; *Queen Isabelle de Bourbon on Horseback* (1632-35) 64; *Queen Margarita of Austria on Horseback* (1628-35) 64; *Doña Jeronima de la Fuente, Nun of Toledo* (before 1622) 43; *Count-Duke Olivares on Horseback* (c. 1638) 15, 63, 67; *Supposed Portrait of Pacheco* (c. 1919-20) 43; *Philip III on Horseback* (1628-35) 64; *Philip IV, full-length portrait* (1625) 47; *Philip IV on Horseback* (c. 1636) 57, 64; *Philip IV* (1655-59) 102, 103;

Miscellaneous: *The Tapestry Weavers (Las Hilanderas*, 1657-60) 102, 104/108, 110; *Las Meninas (The Maids of Honor*, 1656) 6, 96, 110/113; *The Surrender of Breda (The Lances*, before 1635) 14, 58/62;

New York, Metropolitan Museum: *Supper at Emmaus* (c. 1619-20) 38; *King Philip IV* (1624) 45, 47;

New York, Frick Collection: *Philip IV at Fraga* (1644) 16, 68, 78, 83;

New York, Hispanic Society of America: *Astalli-Pamphili* (1650) 19; *Count-Duke Olivares* (1625) 47; *Portrait of a Girl* (c. 1648) 86;

Orihuela, University: *Temptation of St Thomas Aquinas* (c. 1631-32) 54;

Rome, Galleria Doria Pamphili: *Pope Innocent X* (1650) 18, 19, 78, 82/86, 90, 99;

Rouen Museum: *The Geographer* (c. 1628) 76;

Sao Paulo, Museu de Arte: *Portrait of Count-Duke Olivares* (1624) 45, 47;

Seville, San Hermenegildo: *Cristóbal Suárez de Ribera* (1620) 43;

Seville, Archbishop's Palace: *St Ildefonso receiving the Chasuble from the Virgin* (1623) 41/43;

Vienna, Kunsthistorisches Museum: *Prince Baltasar Carlos* (c. 1640) 77, 79; *Infanta Margarita* (c. 1653) 4, 96; *Infanta Margarita* (c. 1653) 94, 96; *Infanta Margarita in a Blue Gown* (1659) 95, 99/101; *Prince Felipe Prosper* (1659) 97/99, *Infanta Maria Teresa* (c. 1653) 92, 93, 101;

Lost Works: *Expulsion of the Moriscoes* (1627) 11, 48; *Portrait of Cardinal Borgia* (c. 1643) 86; *The Prince of Wales* (1623/24) 10; *Portrait of Flaminia Trionfi* (1650) 19; *Don Luis de Fonseca* (1623) 9; *Portrait of Olimpia Maidalchini*

# LIST OF COLORPLATES

# CONTENTS

THIS VOLUME, THE THIRTY-THIRD OF THE COLLECTION "THE TASTE OF OUR TIME", WAS PRODUCED BY THE TECHNICAL STAFF OF EDITIONS D'ART ALBERT SKIRA, FINISHED THE THIRTIETH DAY OF MARCH NINETEEN HUNDRED AND SIXTY TEXT AND ILLUSTRATIONS BY THE

COLOR STUDIO
AT IMPRIMERIES RÉUNIES S.A., LAUSANNE

PLATES ENGRAVED BY GUEZELLE AND RENOUARD, PARIS.

### PHOTOGRAPHS

*Erwin Meyer, Vienna (pages 3, 79, 92, 94, 95, 97, 98, 100, 101, 101a, 101b),*
*Zoltan Wegner, London (pages 6, 12, 15, 31, 33, 36, 37, 41, 42, 49, 51, 53, 57, 58,*
*60, 61, 63, 65, 66, 87, 103, 104, 105, 106, 107, 109, 110, 111, 113), Henry B. Beville,*
*Washington (pages 46, 68), Claudio Emmer, Milan (pages 82, 84, 85). Photographs*
*on pages 52, 71, 72, 73, 74, 80, 81, 91 were obligingly lent by the Magazine* Du*, Zurich.*

PRINTED IN SWITZERLAND